The Great Digital Commission

The Great Digital Commission

Embracing Social Media for
Church Growth and Transformation

Caleb J. Lines

 CASCADE *Books* • Eugene, Oregon

THE GREAT DIGITAL COMMISSION
Embracing Social Media for Church Growth and Transformation

Cascade Books
An Imprint of Wipf and Stock Publishers
199 W. 8th Ave., Suite 3
Eugene, OR 97401

www.wipfandstock.com

PAPERBACK ISBN: 978-1-7252-8784-6
HARDCOVER ISBN: 978-1-7252-8785-3
EBOOK ISBN: 978-1-7252-8786-0

Cataloguing-in-Publication data:

Names: Lines, Caleb J.

Title: The great digital commission : embracing social media for church growth and transformation / Caleb J. Lines.

Description: Eugene, OR: Cascade Books, 2021 | Includes bibliographical references.

Identifiers: ISBN 978-1-7252-8784-6 (paperback) | ISBN 978-1-7252-8785-3 (hardcover) | ISBN 978-1-7252-8786-0 (ebook)

Subjects: LCSH: Social media. | Communication—Religious aspects—Christianity. | Mass media in religion.

Classification: BV4319 .L45 2021 (print) | BV4319 (ebook)

08/18/21

This book is dedicated to my wife, Shawnna, and my daughters, Kit and Rosie, for all of their patience and support through the writing of this book; my parents, Kim and Linda Lines, for their encouragement; and the people of University Christian Church.

Contents

Acknowledgments

THANK YOU TO MY doctoral advisor Dr. Jeff Conklin-Miller for his guidance on the research that led to this book and to Dr. Charles Ess for bringing insights from the field of New Media along the way.

Introduction

The Great Digital Commission

My Church is Dying

I CAN STILL REMEMBER the green shag carpeting and the wood-paneled walls of the rural Missouri congregation in which I spent my formative years. I recall sitting in the second pew from the back—my family's regular spot—and looking up at the stained-glass window behind the baptistry with Jesus' outstretched arms, as if to say, "Follow me." It was in that space that I learned to sing the hymns of the faith. It was there that I learned how wonderful, yet challenging, it is to live in Christian community. It was in that congregation that I learned to ask hard questions and to sit with ambiguous answers. It was there that I heard sermons calling me to work for justice in the world. It was in that seventies-clad worship space where I eventually made the commitment to follow Jesus that would shape the rest of my life. I was baptized under that aforementioned stained-glass window of Jesus with outstretched arms.

This rural Missouri mainline Protestant congregation was never very large, and we were fine with that. It was, however, a congregation that was full of life. There were around eighty to a hundred people on any given Sunday and the wider community saw the congregation as one that made a difference. Over the past several years, that once vibrant, if small, community has been facing steady decline and what seems like an inevitable death. Attendance has decreased significantly; the congregation that once had its limited pews filled, now has fewer than twenty people in worship on a Sunday. They are having to engage in difficult conversations about whether or not they can even keep their doors open. I've returned a few times over the years and it's sad to step foot in the still green-shag-carpeted and wood-paneled sanctuary and look at a congregation without forward momentum. While there are a number of factors that have led to its decline, the congregation has no clear sense of identity, nor a passion for sharing the good news. The people are tired, and the congregation will almost certainly die.

The story of the beloved congregation of my childhood fits into a broader narrative of religious communities around the country, as church attendance decreases and overall religious affiliation continues a sharp decline. According to a 2019 Gallup poll, church membership has declined by nearly 20 percent over the past two decades. In 1999, 69 percent of all Americans were members of a religious community and now only 52 percent are members.[1] Furthermore, the number of people who are not affiliated with any religion in particular, dubbed "nones," has continued to rise, increasing from 8 percent in 1999 to 19 percent now.[2] These statistics can be paired with the Pew Religious Landscape Study, last conducted in 2014, which asks participants with which religious tradition they identify. Pew's study shows that around 70 percent of Americans consider themselves Christian, even if they're not attending services at a church, down from 78 percent in 2007.[3] These statistics have been staggering to those who love the church and don't want to see it die. It's worth noting that in San Diego, where I currently serve, there are more nones than mainline Protestants (by 11 percentage points!).[4]

Those in mainline churches have been wondering about the cause of church decline for decades, as have scholars. Some explanations given include everything from mainliners having fewer

1. Jones, "Church Membership Down."
2. Jones, "Church Membership Down."
3. Pew Research Center, "Religious Landscape Study."
4. Pew Research Center, "San Diego."

children to demographic changes to growing secularization. The truth is that there are likely a number of factors contributing to church decline. But if one thing is clear, it is that most churches have not been able to find a way to reverse the trend. In a recent study, researchers interviewed clergy and congregants across twenty-one denominations in Canada and asked them why mainline churches were declining. While a variety of answers were given, researchers discovered that within declining churches people were more likely to attribute that decline to external factors, while growing churches gave credit for their growth to internal factors. The result was a self-fulfilling prophecy for both sets of congregations. If they believed there was nothing that they could do for church growth, their church attendance continued to decline. If they believed that they could grow their church, they were more likely to be able to do so.[5] The authors of the study also concluded that secularization is the largest reason for decline and that more conservative churches are more "secularization resilient," because their worldview is different enough from the rest of society that coming together becomes more important.[6] Mainliners tend to have a worldview that is very similar—at times, indistinguishable—from secular society. Mainline churches have often failed to clearly articulate what makes them theologically different from other social groups and in many ways have made themselves irrelevant by discarding theology in favor of becoming a social club. When churches have made such a switch, perhaps they deserve to die, because they have lost sight of the radical gospel message. If a church is the same as every other social club, why should it continue to exist? Yet, when mainline congregations recognize the countercultural message of God's inclusive love, radical hospitality, and transformative justice, and embody those values in daily life, it can lead to flourishing community. Fleshing out the values of a congregation and showing how they can lead to growth will be a key focus of chapter 3.

Overall religious affiliation in the US continues declining and churches are closing at alarming rates, yet I wonder if there's

5. Flatt et al., "Secularization and Attribution," 104.
6. Flatt et al., "Secularization and Attribution," 104.

something that churches could do to help stop the decline. For instance, I can't help but wonder how my home congregation in Missouri could expect anything else but decline and closure with zero web presence. There's no webpage. There's no Facebook page. There's not a single photo on Google images. There's not one Yelp or Google review. You can forget about an Instagram or Twitter presence. Other than physically driving by the church, there is no way to find out the time of the service, and there is nothing on the building itself to tell potential visitors anything about what the congregation values. The only way to find out anything about the church is to show up and walk through the doors on a Sunday morning. They believe that because of external forces in society they will decline and close their doors, and *because* of that belief, it will probably come true.

The congregation of my childhood is like so many around the country that have fallen victim to changing times and an inability or unwillingness to change. There was a time when people would simply visit their neighborhood church and where people stayed loyal to denominational affiliation, but times have changed. We are living in an age where fewer people are going to church (or any faith community, for that matter) and many have had terrible experiences of exclusion from churches (the LGBTQ+ community is a case in point). If churches are not actively trying to reach out to their community both by having a physical presence at important community events and a digital presence that communicates their values, they are signing their own death warrants. Churches are closing at rates never before seen and many have felt helpless to actively affect any kind of meaningful change in the trend. Yet, taking seriously the call to share the good news that we find in the Gospels could reinvigorate churches and help them to find a resurrection in the digital age. It is time for churches, especially mainline churches that have been hesitant about evangelism, to embrace the Great Commission.

Introduction

The Great Commission

Go therefore and make disciples of all nations, baptizing them in the name of the Father and of the Son and of the Holy Spirit, and teaching them to obey everything that I have commanded you. And remember, I am with you always, to the end of the age. (Matthew 28:19–20)

The Gospel of Matthew ends with these familiar words of the Great Commission.[7] Going into the world and sharing the good news has been and remains an essential function of all followers of Jesus. Paul Minear points out that an emphasis on making disciples of others was a primary concern from the beginning of Jesus' ministry.[8] In fact, in the Gospel of Matthew, Jesus' first act of public ministry was to recruit Peter, Andrew, James, and John as disciples and encourage them to "fish for people" (Matthew 4:19). Minear emphasizes that when one becomes a follower of Jesus, it means committing to "take up the cross, to lose one's life for his sake, to reduce to secondary status obligations to kinfolk, [and] to refuse to count the cost in advance."[9] This obligation to discipleship within the earliest Christian community continued, even after Jesus had been crucified.

Donald Senior suggests that although much of the Gospel of Matthew has a definitively Jewish tone, that the Great Commission is the moment in the Gospel when the disciples break with the Jewish tradition and become a new movement.[10] This stress on sharing Jesus' message and recruiting new followers is something that was never a large emphasis in the Jewish tradition and shifted the focus of the budding Christian religion, which enabled it to be outwardly focused and to spread extremely quickly. Moreover, building a community that includes all groups and diminishes the importance of distinction between the groups is at the heart of the

7. Other versions can be found in Mark 16:14–18; Luke 24:44–49; Acts 1:4–8; and John 20:19–23.

8. Minear, *Images*, 146.

9. Minear, *Images*, 147.

10. Senior, *Gospel of Matthew*, 73.

evangelistic message. In Galatians 3:28, Paul writes, "There is no longer Jew or Greek, there is no longer slave or free, there is no longer male and female; for all of you are one in Christ Jesus." In creating this kind of community in which barriers between people are broken, we get a glimpse of the reign of God made manifest.

While the disciples began to look outward with the Great Commission, creating a life-transforming community of faith had always been a part of Jesus' core teaching. Throughout the Gospel of Matthew, Jesus emphasizes making disciples and building the reign of God on earth. We see evidence for this in many places in the Gospel, but especially in the Sermon on the Mount. In discussing how Jesus gains disciples while giving the Sermon on the Mount, Richard Lischer suggests that one reason his circle widens is because the real emphasis is on "the corporate dimensions of moral guidance, cure of souls, and the formation of the congregation."[11] Both Jesus and the early apostles used communal life and communal values to build relationships, instead of simply focusing on individual aims. The values of building community and sharing the good news remain relevant today and continue to be effective tools to help people connect with God, especially in a society that tends to focus far too much on individualism.

Nurturing community is one of the most authentic expressions of Jesus' ministry that the church can embody. Yet, it can be difficult to create real, lasting community in our hypermobile world, something that the chapters that follow will explore at length. However, modern technology has given us the tools to connect with people all over the world and to develop and maintain relationships across diverse lines to better fulfill the Great Commission.

Identifying the Problem

While evangelism remains an extremely important focus of the Christian tradition, the mainline church has often failed to keep up with a rapidly changing society, which has limited its ability to

11. Lischer, "Sermon on the Mount," 164.

reach out to new people. Technology is developing at an incredible rate and churches have not been able to keep pace. Although there was a time when all a church needed to do was to open its doors on Sunday morning, those days are long past and churches must become innovative in how they will reach out to new people. The largest problem that the church, especially the mainline Protestant church, is facing today is how to effectively communicate its message and live into the calling of the Great Commission when people see religion, church, and even the Bible as irrelevant.

In *The Luminous Dusk,* Dale Allison discusses the future of books, generally, and the Bible, specifically. He admits that it is often difficult for him to read books uninterrupted without longing to watch TV, yet our attention spans have only gotten shorter since he wrote his book in 2006. He believes that even with changes in the way that people relate to books, the Bible is still worth reading. He says, "The inexplicable divine mystery still speaks through the old pages and through my hermeneutical confusion; and in the end I must pursue the book because it has always pursued me."[12] His statement certainly resonates with me, but I think that the way that people relate to the Bible and religion has changed over the past few decades (and even since 2006). Now the Bible and religion, itself, must be made approachable in new ways for people who have come to see the Bible and organized religion as irrelevant or offensive.

One of the ways that churches have tried to draw people in, especially over the course of the last century, has been by marketing themselves. It's no secret that traditional forms of church marketing (or at least the practices that have been normative over the past several decades) are no longer effective in American society. Churches cannot expect people to read ads in newspapers or yellow pages, to show up on Sundays just because the church is close to their house, or to worship simply because the church has a funny sign outside. In fact, even traditional forms of media such as television and radio have seen a substantial decline in social relevance. While personal invitations to church from those with

12. Allison, *Luminous Dusk,* 111.

whom we are in authentic relationships are still extremely valuable, people have tended to want less to do with organized religion. It's unfortunate that mainline churches have often provided inadequate formation for congregants, so that they might be able to share their faith with more confidence. Additionally, we are living in a much more religiously pluralistic nation than that to which the mainline church has grown accustomed and we must embrace our new reality.

For this reason, it has become incredibly important for churches to invest time, energy, and finances into online and social media. The secular world has long accepted that social media is here to stay and is ever-changing. Unfortunately, many congregations have seen the internet as an impediment instead of the greatest opportunity to fulfill the Great Commission that Christians have ever had available to them. If churches embrace online and social media, their impact on people's lives and on the world can increase dramatically. Yet, in her book *The Social Media Gospel*, Meredith Gould suggests that churches must be strategic in the ways that they approach their digital presence. She states, "[Saying that] 'we need to use social media because everyone else uses it' is not a strategy. Social media is a tool that must be selected and used with purposeful forethought."[13] This includes having a clear sense of identity and mission.

For many churches, the discussion has been about whether they even *should* have a website or a Facebook page. In fact, there has been quite a bit of resistance to having a digital presence within many faith communities. Gould suggests that many people (and church people, in particular) tend to be resistant to social media, because they are afraid that it is isolating and detracts from real, authentic relationships.[14] While there does seem to be evidence that certain types of social media usage can lead to depression and feelings of isolation (an issue I will explore at length in chapter 1),[15] for Gould (and within my own life) relationships have often been

13. Gould, *Social Media Gospel,* 40.

14. Gould, *Social Media Gospel,* 24.

15. Primack et al., "Social Media Use."

enhanced and grown deeper through intentional use of social media. Perhaps a large part of the fear results from the demographic makeup of the mainline church, which is a predominately an older population. Yet, I have seen people from older generations find life-giving affirmation from being involved in different aspects of social media. For instance, homebound members of our church are now able to watch videos of the service and interact with the church through social media, instead of depending entirely on monthly printed newsletters or visits from members of the congregation.

While much has been written about how social media can be optimized for the business world, relatively little has been researched on how churches can effectively spread the gospel online. That is the project of this book. In the last part of the Great Commission, Jesus, knowing that he has just given the disciples an incredibly difficult task, realizes that they will likely need encouragement. As such, he states, "And remember, I am with you always . . ." (v. 20). Surely this also applies to online manifestations of the church. Since the mainline church continues to decline, yet has an incredibly powerful tool at its fingertips, more work needs to be done to resource the church to reach new people through social media. In our time, we should hear a Great Digital Commission.

With the COVID-19 pandemic, most congregations have begun to realize that online options for worship and connection are absolutely necessary, even if they had to be dragged into the twenty-first century kicking and screaming. Those that embraced the Great Digital Commission early likely have had a much easier time adapting to the challenges of worshiping and connecting only online. However, this book will help all congregations think about moving forward with intentionality whether they've been online for years or are brand new to the digital world. Social media is not going anywhere, and all congregations ought to embrace it. However, there is real value in gathering as a physical community that is difficult to replicate in digital spaces. Social media is a tool that can connect people with others and with God, but it is a means, not an end.

Defining Terms

We talk a great deal about social media in our society, yet we rarely take the time to clarify exactly what we mean. Media that is consumed online has been dubbed *new media*, of which social media is one component. One of the challenges in talking about new media is that there are daily developments and advancements. Unlike traditional forms of media (like newspapers, radio, or television), which have remained relatively static, new media is ever-evolving. This, of course, means that definitions of these new forms of media evolve as changes occur. Some have tried to define social media too narrowly by limiting it to specific platforms that are currently being utilized. Others have such breadth that virtually anything online could be considered social media.

For the purpose of this book, a simple definition that allows for changes in technology is the most helpful. Therefore, in the chapters that follow, I will use the following definition of *social media*: social media consists of applications and websites that enable social networking and the creation/sharing of digital content. Perhaps the easiest way to tell the difference between social media and other forms of digital media is whether or not people have to interact with each other in order for it to have value. To put it another way: without the creation of content and interaction with others, social media doesn't exist. This separates church social media accounts from media forms like websites, because it is the interaction with content that is key.

In addition to new media, I will also draw upon the field of *digital religion*. There is now an entire field of study focused on digital religion with many definitions, but perhaps the most helpful definition comes from Heidi Campbell. She says, "We can think of digital religion as a bridge that connects and extends online religious practice and spaces into offline contexts, and vice versa."[16] Digital religion scholars recognize that what people do online and what people do offline are related, including how they think about, relate to, and engage with religion. Examining this connection

16. Campbell, ed., *Digital Religion*, 4.

throughout the following chapters will be key for understanding how churches that exist in the physical world can create content that helps people to connect online and find their way into real-life pews.

I will also focus on both *evangelism* and *marketing*. Evangelism is, of course, sharing the good news in the hopes that others might share in the beloved community of God's realm. Marketing, on the other hand, is the way that individual churches portray themselves in the hopes of attracting people to the congregation. While church marketing can lead to evangelism, it's important to note the difference between the two. This difference will be explored at length in the following chapter.

Throughout this book, I will use a number of terms with specific theological meanings. While some of these definitions may seem clear, it's important to state clearly how I will apply each throughout the book. *The church* refers to the universal church and Christianity as a whole. A *congregation* is a local manifestation of the universal church (*a* church, not *the* church). A *community* is a place where people have certain characteristics in common. While there is often overlap between these three terms, they are, in fact, different. The church refers to all Christians both past and present. Christian congregations belong to the church, but discussing characteristics of an individual congregation is different than traits that can be applied universally to all Christians. Likewise, the term *community* can be used to refer to a congregation, because people within a congregation necessarily have certain traits in common (i.e., meeting in the same sanctuary and participating in the same rituals), but it can also be used in a broader sense to refer to people who are connected to a congregation digitally.

In addition to a community that simply shares traits in common, in the pages that follow I will also be exploring what is involved in creating *authentic community*. I define authentic community as a community where people can be fully themselves, yet also grow through the nurture and challenge of others. Authentic community is different than a simple gathering of people with certain common traits. When the church is at its best, it forms authentic communities where people are fundamentally accepted, yet also challenged to grow into fuller relationship with God and one another. While authentic community can likely be created in certain online spaces, authentic community is most likely to develop in a physical space. As will be demonstrated in the next chapter, social media that reflects authentic community can bring people into congregations and lead to church growth.

— *Chapter One* —

Ups and Downs of Social Media

Introduction

Social media is an extremely powerful tool that congregations can utilize to help people experience God's radical love. This chapter argues that while social media is absolutely essential for church growth and vitality in the twenty-first century, it also comes with real challenges. Congregations must embrace social media intentionally and be aware of the effects that it has on mental health, community connection, and religious authority. If church leaders are prepared to think theologically about these issues, congregations can not only bring people into their pews, but can also help to combat much of the negativity and isolation that comes with social media.

I Found You Online!

"It's been a long time since I've been to a church." This is one of the most common phrases that I hear when people walk through the doors of our congregation. The church that I serve is in the Hillcrest neighborhood of San Diego, which is the historic LGBTQ+ neighborhood. In fact, our congregation sits only two blocks from the LGBT Community Center, where a giant pride flag fills the sky. Summertime Pride celebrations are always the busiest times in the neighborhood around the church. In 1994, the church shut the gates to the parking lot during the Pride celebration and an interim minister told them that if they continued to close their gates (literally and metaphorically) the church would die. The church opened its eyes and noticed who their neighbors were and began to feel God tugging on their hearts to become more welcoming. The next year, they began participating in Pride and by 1999 had voted to become the first Open and Affirming congregation of the Christian Church (Disciples of Christ) in all of Southern California. This vote meant that they would explicitly welcome all people regardless of sexual orientation or gender identity into the full life and leadership of the church. This was a game changer for the congregation, because it meant that people who had felt excluded from church now had a faith community in the neighborhood that they could call home.

More than twenty years later, one of the great joys of pastoring this church is when people begin attending after a long absence from organized religion or having never been part of a church. Fortunately for me, this happens frequently, despite the narrative of church decline. Given our location, there are many people who find their way to our congregation after spending years away from anything remotely religious. Many people come to us because we are explicitly welcoming to all. A common story that I hear from visitors is that they loved the church of their childhood, but they were rejected because of their sexual orientation or gender identity. This caused them to want little to do with organized religion, because they have felt ostracized. They also often feel like churches are not safe places for them to enter, because of their experience. There are a lot of churches that claim to be "open" but really have more of a don't ask, don't tell policy. Once people see that there is a church that will really accept them for who they are, they tend to feel a great sense of relief.

What does all this have to do with social media? A lot, as it turns out. Through targeted social media usage, our church has been able to reach people who have felt marginalized. Social media has been a tool to show people how our church is living as an authentic community of welcome, love, and hospitality. That's why the most common answer I get when asking how people discovered our church is "I found you online!" In our case, being open and affirming is a crucial part of our identity. Showing that we "practice what we preach" has been important for people who want to see if we are authentic in our message. The same is true no matter what a church says about themselves. Social media can be a powerful tool to help potential churchgoers see if a church really views the world the way that it claims. What a church posts on social media (and what members say about a church online) tells people a lot about whether a church is really an authentic place. In my experience, social media has been a place where people who are curious about religion and church can check it out and see if it is a place where they really might fit in.

Our church has a strong web presence and we have invested significant time, energy, and, yes, money, into our social media; it has paid off. This wasn't always the case, however. When I arrived at my current congregation in 2015, there were multiple issues. Our website was more than ten years old and certainly looked its age. We had a Facebook page, but it had only been used sporadically and with little strategic thought. I discovered that we had a live Twitter feed with old branding, and no one could figure out the login information. There were occasional videos of worship posted on YouTube, but they were all of poor quality. Needless to say, our online presence was in need of an overhaul.

The congregation had been working with a web designer on a new website, but it had been in a beta version for two years and it already looked outdated. Instead of making that site live, we opted for a service that operated on templates, so that the church could easily update information, as well as the look and feel of the site. We began using our Facebook page intentionally and daily. We got rid of the Twitter feed with old branding. We updated our Google+ profile (when that service was still around) and started a LinkedIn profile. We expanded to Instagram and began to post daily. We eventually hired a part-time videographer to livestream our services to Facebook and YouTube, to post edited versions of the service on YouTube, and to create highlight clips for Instagram. We also began using our videographer to do promo videos.

We have tried to diversify our reach, because, as Meredith Gould says in her book *The Social Media Gospel*, "Your audiences are using multiple platforms, at different times, and for different reasons."[1] Moreover, she suggests that use of social media platforms can be divided by generation. With older generations (Silent and Baby Boomer) using Facebook and blogs and younger generations (Millennial and Gen Z) using Instagram, Snapchat, Twitter, and YouTube, and the middle generation (Generation X) using a wide variety of platforms.[2] This means that a church really should operate on more than one platform, should adapt content to appeal to the generation that is using a particular platform, and should have a target audience in mind.

Social media has been an important tool for our congregation and many others. While I think social media is a reality that can benefit churches if it is embraced and used appropriately, there are realities about which churches must be aware when considering the use of social media. Social media use can backfire if it isn't consistent with who the church claims to be. If not used carefully, church social media can also contribute to problems instead of helping to alleviate them. This chapter will acknowledge and explore the downsides to social media, while highlighting the potential to address these concerns and quell church decline.

Challenges with Social Media

It's no secret that many churches have been somewhat reluctant to embrace social media. To be clear, there are some good reasons to be wary. There is a widespread belief that social media usage can lead to depression and feelings of isolation and there is also some research to back up these fears. For instance, the National Institute for Mental Health conducted a study of 1,787 adults ages nineteen

1. Gould, *Social Media Gospel*, 43.
2. Gould, *Social Media Gospel*, 17.

to thirty-two. Their conclusion was that "[Social media] use was significantly associated with increased depression."[3] However, by their own acknowledgement, while most young adults (90 percent) use social media, "Published studies on the association between social media use and depression have yielded mixed results" and "multiple factors contribute to depression."[4] According to this research, it is difficult to tell whether social media is primarily responsible for an increase in depression in young adults or if social media is only one of a number of factors contributing to increased levels of depression. Nonetheless, it does seem likely that certain types of social media usage can negatively impact one's health.

Another study divided participants into five groups based on the amount of time they spent using social media and found that the two groups that used social media the most "were associated with the most risk of depression and anxiety."[5] The authors suggest this may be linked to the fact that individuals who use social media the most routinely update their status and check for "likes." The obsession with seeing how others react "may lead to depression if the individual does not receive the desired feedback from his or her social media audience."[6] Clearly, this can also lead to anxiety, since people are worried about how they are being perceived on social media and if their posts are popular enough.

Depression among young adults seems to be connected to what scholars call "perceived social isolation," which refers to how isolated one feels from others. In a 2017 study, researchers found that "young adults with high SMU [social media usage] seem to feel more socially isolated than their counterparts with lower SMU."[7] Brian Primack, a co-author of the aforementioned studies, was somewhat surprised by the findings, saying, "It's social media, so aren't people going to be socially connected?"[8] Multiple studies

---

3. Sidani et al., "Social Media Use," 323.
4. Sidani et al., "Social Media Use," 323.
5. Primack et al., "Use and Depression."
6. Primack et al., "Use and Depression."
7. Primack et al., "Perceived Social Isolation."
8. Hobson, "Feeling Lonely?"

have confirmed that face-to-face social interactions have a positive impact on mental health, but it seems that digital relationships can have the exact opposite effect, leading to feelings of loneliness and isolation.[9] As Primack suggests, this is counterintuitive. If people are more connected, shouldn't they feel better and less isolated?

Drawing on the work of Barry Wellman, new media scholar Lori Kendall argues that there is a distinction between "community" and the "networked individualism" that often occurs online.[10] Wellman suggests that there has been a societal shift occurring in developed nations since the 1960s:

> People remain connected, but as individuals rather than being rooted in the home bases of work unit and household. Individuals switch rapidly between their social networks. Each person separately operates his [or her] networks to obtain information, collaboration, orders, support, sociability, and a sense of belonging.[11]

Wellman also suggests that "the proliferation of the Internet both reflects and facilitates the shift."[12] The shift has been kicked into high gear since the advent of social media. Kendall suggests that compared to networked individualism, "community," on the other hand, "evokes empathy, affection, support, interdependence, consensus, shared values, and proximity."[13]

A society built on networked individualism means that instead of depending on one network, as people have for most of human history, we now have multiple networks to which we relate in different ways depending upon our needs. With the advent of the internet, broadly, and social media, specifically, each person's networks have grown exponentially. Yet, members of the network often include people who have never met face to face. The concept of networked individualism reinforces why people often feel

9. Hobson, "Feeling Lonely?"
10. Kendall, "Community and the Internet," 311.
11. Wellman, "Little Boxes," 5.
12. Wellman, "Little Boxes," 1.
13. Kendall, "Community and the Internet," 309.

isolated when online. People are connected to each other, but most online spaces do not adequately facilitate those values that Kendall suggests are often associated with community: empathy, affection, support, interdependence, consensus, shared values, and proximity. Think, for example, of the dreaded comment section, after any online article or social media post. People can post any response they want (often anonymously) and have no fear of losing any real relationships. There is no need to be kind or to use any filtered language. Even though people can speak to (or at) each other, there is no relationship on which the exchange is built. True community is based on accountability and relationship and if those are not carefully curated online, it's easy to see how interactions could lead to feelings of isolation rather than connection.

Negative impacts on our health are not only caused by people with whom we have no offline relationship, however. One of the realities of social media is that we often get only a snapshot of people's lives using the filter of their choosing. Seeing seemingly perfect lives on social media can have a negative impact on mental health. Psychologist Ethan Kross studies the effect of social media on mental health and suggests, "Envy is being taken to an extreme" as we see "photoshopped lives," and "that exerts a toll on us the likes of which we have never experienced in the history of our species. And it is not particularly pleasant."[14]

Psychologist Rachel Andrew suggests that social media has made everyone's life available for comparison, no longer just those in our immediate vicinity, and we have chosen to carry the devices that enable comparisons in our pockets every hour of the day.[15] It's important to note that presenting oneself positively in physical communities has always been done, yet social media makes it easier and accessible to everyone.[16] Living in a state of constant

14. Sarner, "The Age of Envy."

15. Sarner, "The Age of Envy."

16. Erving Goffman was the first to analyze the phenomenon of people presenting themselves favorably, which he did in his 1959 book *The Presentation of Self in Everyday Life.*

envy not only affects one's quality of life and mental health, it also limits our ability to be grateful to God for what we have.

Social media can also have impacts on a person's theology. I come from a tradition that emphasizes "responsible freedom of belief" in biblical interpretation, meaning that through study and community accountability people are responsible for developing their own theology. In fact, one of the early rallying cries of the founders of the Restorationist movement was "No creed but Christ, no book but the Bible, no law but love."[17] Yet, there is not necessarily communal accountability in the digital world, which can lead to a dangerously hyper-individualized theology. Many church leaders have been particularly concerned about the way that theology is developing outside of what has been considered orthodox Christian belief.

Of course, the concern about a hyper-individualized theology vs. orthodoxy may have more to do with the authority of religious leaders than a concern about keeping religious orthodoxy. In writing about religious authority in the digital age, Pauline Hope Cheong notes that "the Internet is viewed as a danger to religious authority because it presents potentially oppositional information that negatively affects the credibility of religious institutions and leadership."[18] It's certainly true that as people have greater access to more resources, their theological understanding is likely to be broader. I'm inclined to believe that this is mostly a good thing, except that many congregants may not be able to adequately discern whether a source is legitimate, which could lead to a theology built on opinions outside both the scholarly consensus and what is typically acceptable within Christian community or even their own local church community.

Cheong states, "The spread of unorthodox teaching calls attention to the possible weakening of the status of religious leaders as spiritual mentors."[19] Again, this is not necessarily a bad thing, except that religious leaders have tended to be the ones who have

17. Blowers et al., eds., *Stone-Campbell Movement*, 688.

18. Cheong, "Authority," 76.

19. Cheong, "Authority," 76.

done years of academic study to help guide the spiritual lives of a congregation. Perhaps this is why a popular meme has arisen on social media amongst clergy. The meme is a picture of a coffee cup with the words "Please Don't Confuse Your Google Search With My Theology Degree."

With all of these negative aspects of social media usage, one might wonder why churches should use it at all. Shouldn't churches take a stand against something that is clearly having a negative impact on people's health and, perhaps, their faith? In a TED Talk titled "Connected, but Alone?," Sherry Turkle advocates a controlled use of technology in our lives. She says, "I'm not suggesting that we turn away from our devices, just that we develop a more self-aware relationship with them, with each other, and with ourselves."[20] I believe this is the approach that churches should take. Churches need to be aware of the risks of social media, yet also recognize that their digital presence can be a positive force to help combat online negativity and perceived isolation, both of which can lead to depression and anxiety. Moreover, in thinking about the use of media strategically, churches should certainly be a part of helping people think about how they are engaging with both their devices and social media. Pastors should be thinking theologically about social media, too. Church leaders can help congregants to think about social media as a tool for sharing their faith and helping people to connect with the congregation.

It's also important to note that while the statistics cited in this chapter represent real experience, each of the studies states that there were a number of people participating who had *the exact opposite* experiences of social media. There were people who connected with others they'd never met face to face and formed real friendships. There were people who felt lonely in their offline lives but were able to develop true community online. There were people who found a way to combat depression by having access to a network of people who have had the same lived experiences as them. There were certainly people—like the ones who found their way to our congregation—who discovered a theology online

20. Turkle, "Connected, but Alone?"

that was liberating. So these studies represent general trends, not every person's experience, but they certainly raise issues of which churches should be aware.

Combating Congregational Decline

A few years ago, I was at a denominational conference where one of the speakers was lecturing on causes of mainline Protestant church decline. The top two reasons he cited were that mainliners were having fewer children and society was increasingly secular. While these causes may have been true, it seemed like an unhelpful assessment that left church decline to factors that were completely out of our control. As noted in the introduction, attributing decline entirely to outside sources is something that mainline Protestants have tended to do. While these factors may be real, one of the reasons for church decline is certainly that most churches have not been able to find a way to be relevant to our modern society. Nothing speaks to irrelevance more than simply being absent from a place where most people are already. This is not to say that the church needs to embrace all elements of contemporary society, but rather that if we want to reach people and bring them into local congregations, we must use tools like social media to reach them.

As noted earlier, as social media ages and more studies are done on the impact of social media on long-term mental health, we continue to learn that there are certainly downsides to social media usage. Churches should be cognizant of the negative aspects of social media and try to confront them where possible. However, one simple fact remains: most people are on social media and will continue to use it whether or not churches embrace it. In fact, social media usage continues to increase. When the Pew Research Center began tracking social media usage in 2005, only 5 percent of American adults used it. That number climbed to 50 percent by 2011 and is now at 72 percent.[21] These numbers indicate that social

---

21. Pew Research Center, "Social Media Fact Sheet."

media usage is no longer just for the younger generations, but is a reality for all ages in the US.

While it's understandable that many churches want to take a stand against the negative impacts of social media, avoiding it altogether is denying the reality that most congregants are already using social media. However, if churches enter the social media sphere with intentionality, they could positively impact people's lives and help to counter the negative effects that social media has had on some people. It's also true that people are looking online to help meet their spiritual needs. The Barna Group found that more people across the generations are using the internet as a resource to read the Bible and enrich their faith.[22] If a church makes the decision to be disengaged from the internet and social media, they are leaving their members on their own to discover spiritual resources online.

Meredith Gould argues, "Until very recently, when worship attendance started declining in just about every Christian denomination, church leadership didn't have to think strategically about much of anything except maybe fund-raising and overflow seating for the annual Christmas pageant."[23] Of course, things have changed and in order to combat church decline, churches now need to be strategic about almost everything to ensure that they do not end up closing their doors. Since most people are now on social media, it is clearly an arena with which churches ought to be strategic. Scholar Christopher Helland states, "Many people using the Internet no longer distinguish between life-online and life-off-line—rather, being 'online' has become part of their daily life and social existence."[24] People expect to be able to connect with the same institutions online with which they are able to connect offline, including their faith community. Moreover, since people no longer distinguish between the two spheres as they once did, what happens online is just as valid as what happens offline.

22. Barna Group, "State of the Bible 2017."

23. Gould, *Social Media Gospel*, 39.

24.. Helland, "Ritual," 25.

Interestingly, surprisingly little research has been done on how increased strategic social media usage has affected church growth. This is mind-boggling considering that it is the most powerful tool to spread the gospel that humanity has ever possessed. Don't believe me? Just think how many people can see a viral post. For a recent sermon series, I did a promo video that reached more than thirty-three times the number of people who sit in our congregation's pews on a Sunday morning. With a little creativity and planning, even small and midsize congregations can have a significant impact in a way that was much more difficult only a few years ago.

The congregation I currently serve grew by 50 percent in a three-year period—a trajectory that continues. There are, of course, a number of factors for this increase, but as I've noted, social media is certainly one of them. Our congregation is not alone. A 2015 study of growing congregations of multiple faiths conducted by the Hartford Institute found that social media is of vital importance, especially for engaging younger adults. The authors state, "Congregations wanting to engage younger adults almost certainly need a basic digital literacy and some kind of web presence to be taken seriously."[25] This is true because "technology is not only a tool, it's a social force that shapes daily life."[26] This is the reality that congregations must realize: social media is shaping the lives of our congregants (and potential congregants) and by not engaging with it, we are choosing to be disengaged from arguably the most important and powerful social force of our time.

In order to be the most effective, social media needs to be used to show what is unique about a congregation. That uniqueness must be true and authentic, but social media helps to amplify the message. The ultimate goal of every church ought to be help people experience God's love, which Jesus has shown to us (evangelism). In order to do that most effectively, churches must embrace certain aspects of modern life without fully capitulating to them. Using social media as a tool to help people realize how a

25. Hartford Institute, *Engaging Young Adults*, 42.
26. Hartford Institute, *Engaging Young Adults*, 43.

congregation is striving to live out the gospel can lead to true evangelism. While it's absolutely correct for a congregation to confront aspects of modern society that are at odds with the gospel, it is inauthentic to the Christian message for a church to turn its back on the society in which it finds itself. It is by knowing a society and offering a hopeful alternative that churches can thrive. Yet, in order for people to know that there is a hopeful alternative, people have to be able to hear the church's message.

In *God's Companions*, Samuel Wells develops a helpful distinction between what he calls "priestly" and "prophetic" evangelism. Priestly evangelism comes in the natural form of congregational life. When people are able to experience God's presence through participation in worship and the mission of the church, they have experienced priestly evangelism. Prophetic evangelism, on the other hand, proclaims the priestly evangelism to the outside world.[27] Applying this understanding of evangelism to how churches can spread the gospel in the twenty-first century is valuable. A church ought to be embodying God's reign in such a way that it is transformative for the congregants both through worship and through the ways that it is impacting its local community, which is its priestly evangelism. A church can use social media as prophetic evangelism—as a way to proclaim the transformative nature of how the congregation is living out the gospel.

Highlighting how a church is living out the gospel in its local context can help people to realize a longing for some deeper spirituality and connection. Unfortunately, so many churches have not effectively shared their experience of how living in Christian community has been transformative. Today, churches no longer have the luxury of sloppy evangelism. Churches must find ways to amplify their message, not only so that they can thrive, but so that the church can transform the world in which we live to a more peaceful and just place. A study conducted by the Hartford Institute found that "congregations that stick out from the crowd are more likely to be growing."[28] Congregations that know who they

27. Wells, *God's Companions*, 57–64.
28. Roozen, "American Congregations," 5.

are and are able to articulate that distinction well are more likely to attract people, because they proclaim something unique. This means that if a congregation wants to both grow numerically and also change the world for the better, it has to have a clear sense of its own identity, a topic which will be discussed at length in chapter 3.

One of the most comprehensive studies that has been done on church social media use was conducted by marketing scholar Marion Stanton Webb in 2012. Webb looked at 1,056 Protestant churches and discovered that church websites helped to attract and retain members, while social media helped to retain members.[29] However, much has changed since 2012 and, as previously noted, about 22 percent more of the population used social media in 2019 than in 2011, so it is very likely that social media has become a tool not only to retain members, but also to attract. The study concludes by stating that since paper marketing is no longer effective, churches "must become proficient in utilizing the most advanced media, tools, and methods."[30] Webb suggests quite bluntly, "Churches need to master the art of marketing and be proactive and creative in their efforts to build and sustain membership."[31]

Churches are beginning to recognize the necessity of an online presence. Among Protestant churches, a 2018 survey found that 84 percent had a website and 84 percent had a Facebook page.[32] Since church membership continues to decline, simply having a web and social media presence is not enough to combat the decline. And of course the study doesn't indicate how churches are using social media, only if they have some presence. The same study found that only 16 percent of churches surveyed had a Twitter account and only 13 percent used Instagram, but the largest churches surveyed utilized both Twitter and Instagram.[33] As noted, Facebook primarily appeals to an older demographic and

29. Webb, "Church Marketing," 68.
30. Webb, "Church Marketing," 80.
31. Webb, "Church Marketing," 83.
32. Lifeway Research, "Pastor Views."
33. Lifeway Research, "Pastor Views."

is used much less frequently by Millennials and Gen Zers. Larger churches also updated their websites more frequently and were actively looking for new technology to reach people.[34] Churches that are larger and growing are not simply *on* social media, they are *investing* time, energy, and money into creating a vibrant, dynamic presence across multiple social media platforms.

Conclusion

Heidi Campbell suggests that "community online serves as a 'supplement, not substitute' for offline church involvement as members [have] joined online communities in order to meet specific relational needs."[35] It is important to note that the research highlighted in this chapter confirms that digital community often cannot fully serve as a substitute for face-to-face community. Churches ought to be using social media as a tool to enhance their offline worshiping community and as an entry point for people new to a particular congregation. It is important for congregations to be aware of the negative impacts that social media can have on the lives of congregants and make an intentional effort to connect people with a face-to-face community. Offline communities can help combat negative impacts of networked individualism such as perceived social isolation, anxiety, and depression.

Social media is essential not only to quell church decline, but also to foster church growth. Congregations need to be living out the gospel within their local community in a way that is transformative and helps people to encounter the incredible gift of knowing the living God. Social media can help people outside of the church learn about what living in Christian community looks like. It can also remind people that while Sunday worship and the day-to-day work of the church ought to be a foretaste of God's reign on earth, congregants have to make an intentional effort to follow the teachings of Jesus in their lives outside of the congregation, as well.

34. Lifeway Research, "Pastor Views."
35. Campbell, "Understanding," 69.

Social media can be an extremely powerful tool to keep the gospel at the forefront of people's minds throughout the week, even in an environment—like on social media—that is all too often negative and overly competitive. In the next chapter, we will examine the types of religious communities that have developed online. Some of these communities are autonomous, while others are connected with a face-to-face offline community. Looking at these different types of online religious communities will help us to understand the ways that Christians are able to proclaim an authentic witness in a digital environment.

Chapter Two

Digital Authenticity

Introduction

CHAPTER 1 ARGUED THAT social media is important for congregational growth and vitality. By embracing social media while fully cognizant of its possible negative impacts, churches can be a powerful force for good online. However, in order for congregations to do so, they must be authentic. The introduction to this book defines an authentic community as one where people can be fully themselves, yet also grow through the nurture and challenge of others. As this chapter will show, we are living in a time when authenticity is more important than ever, especially if congregations want to attract new members. So we will explore what authentic community looks like in digital environments.

In Search of Authentic Community

If you were to walk through New Haven, Connecticut's historic town green on a beautiful Sunday afternoon, you'd see mature elm trees covering the paved paths that cross the grass, as people walk by engaged in casual conversation. You'd notice the large neo-Gothic buildings of Yale University's Old Campus, as study groups sit in circles on the ground. You'd observe the close proximity of three historic churches that fit perfectly into the typical New

England landscape. In many ways, this public square looks exactly the way that you would expect. One sight that might seem oddly out of place, however, is a gathering on the public green behind the large stone Episcopal church. If you were to wander over in curiosity, you'd quickly notice that instead of university students with their heads in books, there are people banging on five-gallon plastic buckets in a makeshift drum circle. Upon closer inspection, you might notice a wooden altar constructed on the frame of a shopping cart and information about homeless services scattered on pop-up tables. As you stood there, people would begin to gather, to chat, and to sing; you would instantly become a part of the community whether or not that was your original intent. This unique ministry is called Chapel on the Green. While the liturgy, location, and structure are designed with people living on the streets specifically in mind, it is open to absolutely everyone. The community consists of people experiencing homelessness, university professors, students, people working in the nearby the financial district, people who walk by and are curious about this oddity, and youth who are volunteering their Sundays to help with the worship and to serve food afterward.

In seminary, I was a part of this community. Its design was based on a model for an outdoor church in Boston called Common Cathedral. The concept of the church is that in order to reach people who live outside, you should go outside and meet people where they are already. Taking ministry to the street shows vulnerability. It shows that the church is willing to leave the sanctuary and go out into the world. At Chapel on the Green, unlikely friendships were built as people learned what it meant to embody the radically inclusive gospel of hospitality and vulnerability. This was made particularly evident during the passing of the peace before the Eucharist. During that time, the diverse group of people gathered for worship shook hands, embraced, and embodied the breaking down of social barriers demanded by the reign of God. The prayers of the people became the most important part of the service, because people took the time to bare their souls and to listen to and pray for each other. When newcomers would see this incredible ministry, they would often comment that it felt like "authentic community."

Chapel on the Green feels authentic, because people are expected to come exactly as they are and are accepted. There's no pretense about coming with addiction or mental illness or homelessness or family problems or dirty clothes; all of these elements that are typically barriers for people coming to church are accepted at Chapel on the Green as normal parts of life. On the other hand, there's also no judgment for people who are doing well financially with a fulfilling career and happy family life. All are welcome to be a part of this unique faith community. This community felt different, it felt authentic, which is why some people who had little use for religion otherwise, found a home in this unlikely outdoor church.[1]

How Can Offline Churches Be Authentic Online?

Drawing on several definitions of authenticity, digital religion scholar Kerstin Radde-Antweiler suggests that people and churches are authentic if "they present themselves as they truly are, in other words if they are not pretending to be someone else or playing another role."[2] Those who are leaving the church consistently state that churches do a poor job of being authentic; they don't live up to the identity they claim. The Barna Group found that of Millennials who don't go to church, 85 percent of them say that the reason they don't go is because the church is hypocritical.[3] As the Barna Group puts it, "To a generation that prides itself on the ability to smell a fake at ten paces, hypocrisy is a worrisome indictment."[4] The church has—or at least is widely perceived to have—an authenticity problem. The late Rachel Held Evans wrote an article about authenticity in the church for *The Washington Post* that garnered quite a bit of attention. In it, she states, "For

1. More information about this community is available at http://chapelonthegreen.weebly.com.

2. Radde-Antweiler, "Authenticity," 88.

3. Barna Group, "What Millennials Want."

4. Barna Group, "What Millennials Want."

a generation bombarded with advertising and sales pitches, and for whom the charge of 'inauthentic' is as cutting an insult as any, church rebranding efforts can actually backfire, especially when young people sense that there is more emphasis on marketing Jesus than actually following Him."[5]

This is the issue with authenticity within the church: people—even people who have little familiarity with the Bible—know that Jesus primarily spoke about love, yet churches seem to have a very difficult time actually practicing that love. For Millennials, at least, the indictment of hypocrisy is likely linked to both perception about the church's stance on LGBTQ+ issues and politics. The same Barna study cited above also found that 91 percent of nonchurch-going Millennials perceived the church as "anti-homosexual."[6] Additionally, churches linked to conservative political ideology often make the news and many see that as incompatible with Jesus' teachings, which are focused on love and acceptance. Put simply, many Americans—especially Millennials—think that the church does a good job of talking about love and a terrible job of actually enacting it in the real world.

Rachel Held Evans had a proposal, however. Instead of trying to make church "cool" churches ought to strive to be authentic places, or as she puts it, we need "to keep worship weird."[7] Evans argues that being reminded of mortality on Ash Wednesday is weird. Being reminded that you are a beloved child of God through the waters of baptism is weird. Feeding the hungry is weird. She says that all of these practices stand out because they are countercultural. That is to say, churches shouldn't portray themselves to be something they are not, nor should churches try to be trendy, just to get people in the pews. Instead, congregations should simply focus more on trying to follow the teachings of Jesus. Social media, then, is not about a self-serving marketing campaign simply to get people into the pews, but rather social media ought to be used to amplify a congregation's "weirdness." It ought to show how

5. Evans, "Want Millennials Back?"

6. Barna Group, "What Millennials Want."

7. Evans, "Want Millennials Back?"

a congregation is living out the values that flow organically from the teachings of Jesus. A congregation should use social media as a way of demonstrating authenticity. There's nothing wrong with highlighting ways that a congregation is making a difference in the world. However, there is a problem whenever the congregation chooses to highlight something that is either inauthentic to who the congregation actually is or inauthentic to the teachings of Jesus.

Amplifying the ways that congregations are making a difference is consistent with Jesus' teachings. In the Gospel of Matthew, Jesus says, "You are the light of the world. A city built on a hill cannot be hid. No one after lighting a lamp puts it under the bushel basket, but on the lampstand, and it gives light to all in the house. In the same way, let your light shine before others, so that they may see your good works and give glory to your Father in heaven" (Matthew 5:14–16). In these verses from the Sermon on the Mount, Jesus gives important instructions about how his followers are to live. Jesus suggests that his followers have an obligation to share their good works, not for bragging rights, but to glorify God. Churches that use social media to inspire, to show how they are making the world a better place, and to empower people to serve God in their own lives are "letting their light shine." If they are living out their professed values (which is the focus of chapter 3), they are displaying authenticity. Is the purpose of a church's social media account to show their new coffee shop, the amenities of their facility, and the size of their congregation? Or is the purpose of their account to show how they are serving God by helping others and deepening the spiritual lives of those who are in attendance? The former reeks of self-serving inauthenticity, while the latter might inspire people to get more involved in the work of the church. In all fairness, though, most churches probably do a bit of both. While my own congregation's feed mostly highlights the work we are doing and strives to articulate our progressive Christian theology, our most viewed video of all time is a video of me disco dancing to promote a sermon on the theology of *Mamma Mia!* Of course, moments like that also let people know about what authenticity looks like in a particular congregation, for better or for worse.

In short, congregations ought to be striving to portray who they really are online, because people will be able to tell whether or not they are being authentic. A congregation needs to be comfortable talking online about who they are and what they value. If a congregation is filled with people over sixty (as most mainline Protestant congregations are), it should highlight the work it is doing within that demographic, rather than trying to market itself as something it isn't in the hopes of reaching a younger demographic. Churches ought to highlight ministries that they do well, so that social media can help those ministries be strengthened. If congregations really want to reach out to younger generations, research indicates that those generations care less about the type of music, technology, and worship style than they do about a church being honest about who they are and practicing the radical inclusion taught to us by Jesus Christ.[8] In fact, two of the most effective ways to reach young people are having a ministry of acceptance (true acceptance into the full life and leadership of the church) of the LGBTQ+ community and an active environmental program.[9] Focusing on these two issues of importance to younger generations and highlighting them on social media would likely do more to bring in young people than a great social media campaign aimed at making a church look hip. Focusing on areas about which young people are passionate and are also in line with a congregation's values generate energy and enthusiasm that is palpable and can lead to church growth across all areas of the church's life.

Churches also ought to be highlighting their work in the world and not just what they're doing internally. Millennials, in particular, want to make a difference in the world. They want to be involved in ways where they are making a significant identifiable impact. In an interview with CNN, former Duke Divinity School dean Greg Jones suggests that young people are tired of having endless debates about the same issues (most of which—like sexual

8. Barna Group, "What Millennials Want."

9. Hartford Institute, *Engaging Young Adults*.

orientation—are no longer issues for the younger generations) and are more interested working in the wider world.[10] This means that many Millennials who don't attend church are not necessarily atheists, they just haven't found a way to engage in institutional religion in a way that feels authentic and meaningful. Jones says, "If it is the case that millennials are less 'atheists' than they are 'bored,' then serious engagements with Christian social innovation, and with deep intellectual reflection (and these two things are connected), would offer promising signs of hope."[11] Indeed, studies consistently find that while the number of atheists and agnostics are growing by small margins, most Americans who have stopped going to church still believe in God and identify as Christians.[12] Since most people who do not attend church still hold Christian beliefs, it would stand to reason that churches are doing a poor job of engaging people in ways that are meaningful. If churches use social media in authentic ways, it can be a step towards relevancy to a group of people who have felt like institutional religion has lost all relevance.

Digital Churches and Authenticity

With all of the issues surrounding authenticity for brick-and-mortar faith communities, it's no wonder that some faith communities online have formed without an offline component. Many clergy and other religious professionals are highly skeptical of religion that exists primarily or exclusively online for fear that congregants will begin to turn to digital sources for matters of faith, especially as fewer people attend church. This reaction by religious leaders is somewhat understandable. Kerstin Radde-Antweiler notes that in the traditional publication process "a strict hierarchy of experts dominates the flow of communication and monitors what information is published."[13] Until the dawn of the digital age, when

---

10. Burke, "Millennials Leaving."
11. Burke, "Millennials Leaving."
12. Burke, "Millennials Leaving."
13. Radde-Antweiler, "Authenticity," 97.

people wanted information on a topic, due to the strict criteria of publishing houses, they could be relatively sure that information was written by an expert in the field. [14] If one does a Google search on a given topic, there is obviously no such guarantee about the results they find. While people have access to more information than ever before and, in theory, could be better informed, people are also more likely than in the past to be reading articles written by authors who are not experts in the field of theology. It is also clear that people often do not check sources for the articles that they read to verify accuracy; the mass misinformation of the 2016 presidential campaign is a case in point. For this reason, it is somewhat understandable that religious leaders might be wary of congregants getting bad information.

While we should all be concerned about misinformation online, the digital world can also be viewed as a place for the liberation of new ideas. Online, religion no longer needs to be mediated by those in religious authority. While this is terrifying for some, for others it is life-giving. As Radde-Antweiler points out, "It is no surprise that most of the critical voices on the question of authenticity come from offline communities, especially authorities in religious institutions."[15] As digital religion scholar Pauline Hope Cheong notes, it is religious leaders and institutions who have the most to lose with the spread of online religious communities, primarily their authority and influence over orthodox beliefs.[16] However, having the freedom to explore theology and different religious beliefs could also serve to deepen one's faith, even if the faith individuals confess begins to stray from what has been considered orthodox in most Christian circles. The possibility of straying from too far from orthodoxy is why it continues to be important to be in community, for it is in community that we mediate the acceptable bounds of orthodoxy. Yet, what constitutes community? We have a relatively clear idea of what community looks like offline and

14. Radde-Antweiler, "Authenticity," 97.

15. Radde-Antweiler, "Authenticity," 99.

16. Cheong, "Authority," 76.

even what makes a community feel authentic, but can authentic community form online?

Since the early days of the internet, people have gathered online for religious purposes. Initially, this mostly took the form of online message boards, but it has evolved greatly since then. There are any number of social media pages and groups for particular religious interests, blogs where people can write about faith topics, podcasts where people can discuss religion, and even virtual reality environments like Second Life where people can create an avatar and interact with other worshipers. Do these environments constitute authentic community? This is an interesting question and the answer most likely depends on how a person interacts with others online. Are relationships being built? Is discussion being facilitated? Are people challenging one another? One of the real blessings of offline community is that even though religious communities often attract similar people, it can still be very difficult to live in community with one another. It is in that living together—and frequently in those awkward moments of disagreement—that we experience Christian community. This kind of community can exist online, but it must be created extremely intentionally.

One interesting trend that Radde-Antweiler notes is that online faith communities focused on worship often mirror traditions that one might find offline. Even in virtual communities, like Second Life (where users have avatars), the users manipulate their avatars in ways that are familiar to worshipers, like sitting in virtual pews, lighting virtual candles, and bowing virtual heads. She states, "The user is provided with a feeling of familiarity that gives them security and allows them through the mediated symbolism to 'participate in their perceived authenticity.'"[17] Therefore, online users are still able to engage in meaningful rituals, even if they are not physically a part of them. Radde-Antweiler further suggests, "Religious performances and experiences online generate effects that are not limited to the online arena."[18] Even though these religious practices are digital, they still have meaning in people's

17. Radde-Antweiler, "Authenticity," 92.
18. Radde-Antweiler, "Authenticity," 95.

offline lives. According to Second Life, there are twenty-five faith communities in existence on their site.[19]

Since there are so few faith communities that have actively embraced an entire virtual world like Second Life, perhaps a more relevant example of digital community is online streaming of worship services, which in some ways mirrors what happens in a virtual world. Whenever churches livestream a worship service, people are able to at least observe worship and perhaps engage in meaningful ways. For instance, if someone is curating the feed, virtual visitors can be acknowledged in the physical service, prayer requests can be taken and lifted up, songs can be sung, and people can engage at least in some way with the offline community. On our own congregation's livestream, members frequently share the stream on their own Facebook pages at the beginning of the service and engage with friends in different physical locations who comment on the elements of the service. When people on the livestream feed have prayer requests, members of physical congregation often comment that they are holding the online concern in prayer. So, while these are digital rituals, they clearly have significance in an offline context, as well, which makes them authentic.

There are also places online where no offline community is formed. One clear example of this is a social media page that has been created and is not linked to a physical faith community. To examine this, let's take a closer look at a Facebook page that I've been a fan of for years, "The Christian Left." As of July 2020, the page is just a few thousand fans shy of 400,000, which makes it just slightly smaller than my own entire denomination, the Christian Church (Disciples of Christ).[20] This Facebook page frequently shares articles on theology, social justice, faith positions on political issues, etc. In fact, the page even has T-shirts that you can buy. On their "Our Story" section they say the following:

> On rare occasions people ask, "Why do you guys make such a big deal about this? It's just a Facebook page where you post news articles." No it isn't. This is a ministry, a

19. Second Life, "Spirituality and Belief."
20. Gryboski, "Disciples of Christ."

community, a haven, a hub, and the biggest gathering place in the world where Christian progressives and their allies can gather 24/7/365 and discuss the issues of the day, support one another, offer comfort, share hopes and dreams, ask for advice, share struggles, talk about God anytime we want without being harassed, and learn from the content and from each other how to adopt the teachings of Jesus as a daily path we can follow him on as he instructed us to do. We can also observe and discuss the contrast of not following Jesus in culture and politics.[21]

In this case, I can safely say that I have never intentionally gathered as a part of "The Christian Left" offline community. There is no offline community, as such. However, I have had conversations with friends and colleagues about articles and information that the page has shared. I have also had friends who have purchased and worn the T-shirts. Are we a part of the community? The page, itself, explicitly states that it is both a ministry and a *community*. An argument can be convincingly made that sharing multiple posts a day to such a large audience has an enormous impact on theology and thus, this online community without an existing offline component still acts as community for those who use it as such.

Meredith Gould suggests that "virtual community is real community."[22] Further, she specifically states, "I've witnessed and been privileged to participate in conversations whose authenticity, poignancy, intelligence, faithfulness, and laugh-out-loud humor are as equal to any I've encountered in so-called 'real life.'"[23] If it's true that community can really be fostered online, then maybe her claim is true that "church is no longer confined to or contingent upon a building."[24] Still, it seems that for true community to form there must be an active willingness for relationship-building to happen amongst the participants who are engaging. Of course, the

---

21. The Christian Left, "Our Story."
22. Gould, *Social Media Gospel*, 40.
23. Gould, *Social Media Gospel*, 92.
24. Gould, *Social Media Gospel*, 92.

same can be said for anyone who participates in a brick-and-mortar church. There are plenty of people who just go to church and sit in the pews on Sunday morning. They don't stay afterward for coffee hour. They don't participate in outreach ministries. They don't have friends within the congregation. Are these worshipers more a part of a community than digital members of an online community simply because they have entered into a physical location?

Perhaps what truly defines authentic community is the way in which people engage. If people put forth the effort to get to know others and build relationships (whether they be online or face to face), they are engaging in community; they are participating as a part of the body of Christ. There is real value to meeting face to face, because community often happens naturally through elements of a worship service like the passing of the peace or waiting for the service to start and chatting with your neighbor or speaking with the greeter at the front door or being forced to chat with the pastor as you leave the sanctuary. But with effort on the part of both the person curating a social media account and the participants, authentic community can be created online, even if it looks different than it would with a physical congregation.

An Argument for Physical Communities

I'm an avid user of social media. I belong to several religious social media accounts on various social media platforms that exist without an offline component. Not a day has gone by in the past several years that I haven't checked in on these accounts, and I regularly engage with other people on them. I read articles posted on these platforms, then I comment and share. I frequently have conversations and occasionally disagreements about theological ideas with other digital community members. Additionally, I also follow online accounts of brick-and-mortar communities. I watch with interest in and often admiration for what they are doing. I frequently listen to sermons and lectures, and I find myself intellectually and spiritually enriched by them. I have even joked with other people that certain churches that I've only ever attended digitally are where I go to church once my worship leadership is done on Sunday mornings. However, truth be told, no matter how much I have been enriched by both exclusively online and the digital presence of traditional faith communities, neither compares to the relationships I build in offline communities. While I am an avid supporter of the digital world, it's simply not the same as real living connection, rather, it's an entry point, not the destination. I think that many churches that had to switch to exclusively online worship during COVID-19 physical distancing would agree with this assessment!

Over the past several years, many of my professional connections have been made digitally before I ever meet someone in person. Someone adds me on a social media platform or vice versa and we begin learning about each other's lives, because all of a sudden, we're in each other's lives virtually every day. Whenever I meet that person in real life, I have context for knowing them. When I meet them, I begin asking myself a series of questions. Does this person speak the way I thought they would? Are they who they present themselves to be on social media? What is their personality like offline? I have a baseline knowledge about the person and can more easily engage in small talk (which may well be why introverts often love to meet people on social media before meeting them offline). In short, social media serves as an introduction to who a person is before meeting them and after meeting them it serves as a way to deepen the relationship. Social media works the same way for faith communities.

Social media is often the first point of contact for people when learning about a church. A 2016 Pew Research Study found that 60 percent of Millennials investigated a church online before visiting.[25] However, according to the same survey, it wasn't the digital media that kept them there, rather it was the preaching and whether they felt welcomed by the community.[26] As Pew put it, "Looking for information online may be growing more common, especially among young people and those who have looked for a

25. Masci, "What Do Americans Look For."
26. Pew Research Center, "Choosing a New Church."

congregation recently. But online information still appears to be far less important to potential congregants than experiencing the atmosphere of the congregation firsthand."[27] Online introductions to churches are becoming increasingly important and the number of people who visit churches digitally before stepping foot onto a church's physical campus has very likely only grown since the study was conducted. However, this study also shows that even younger people who are visiting churches still want what people have traditionally expected from faith communities: good sermons and a warm welcome.

Even though the Pew study was focused on people who were specifically looking for an offline community, it indicates some important truths for brick-and-mortar churches. First, they must invest in digital media, because more and more people are going online before visiting. Second, they cannot rely solely on digital media. Digital media should a be a tool to reach new people, but once they're in the doors, churches should focus on what they already know how to do: create meaningful worship and ensure that new people feel welcomed. Third, social media can serve as an important follow-up tool, because many of the visitors have already engaged with the church online. If a specific effort is made during the service to get people to follow the church on social media, then the church has an instant place in someone's life. In fact, if that person had a pleasant experience, seeing posts throughout the next week can serve as a reminder of Sunday's experience and make them more likely to return.

While people can potentially have their spiritual needs met in an entirely digital environment, there is often still a longing for a physical space to gather, too. Authentic community can develop in digital spaces apart from physical communities and in some cases, this has clearly led to deepening spirituality and an identification with a digital ministry as one's primary religious conduit. While these cases are very interesting, it doesn't mean that every church should be striving to create an exclusively online community. Quite the opposite is true. While churches must have a digital presence,

27. Pew Research Center, "Choosing a New Church."

their primary ministry ought to be in the real world. As articulated in the previous chapter, relying solely on the digital world can lead to networked individualism rather than true community and can cause people to feel more isolated and depressed. Any exclusively digital communities ought to be aware of this trend and, if they take their role as a spiritual community seriously, strive to actively develop community that connects people on a deeper level both in person and online.

Churches that exist solely online often replicate what happens offline and in theory could replace them and surely have for some. However, as online church scholar Tim Hutchings points out, "Research into religious media, from radio and television to Internet, has consistently reported that audiences use mediated resources to augment local activity."[28] An early Pew study on church usage confirmed this, stating, "The most active online Religion Surfers (those who go online at least several times a week for spiritual material) are also the most active offline participants in their faiths . . . [T]he Internet is a useful supplemental tool that enhances their already-deep commitment to their beliefs and their churches, synagogues, or mosques."[29] So while there are faith communities that exist solely online, it is very likely that most of the active participants are also people who are actively engaged in an offline faith community.

In *Evangelism After Christendom,* Bryan Stone makes the point that in order for a Christian community to really be the church, it must embody the reign of God and proclaim that there is a "radical new order that comes to put an end to the age-old patterns of wealth and poverty, domination and subordination, insider and outsider that are deeply engrained in the way that we relate to one another on this planet."[30] Further, he says, "In order for that new order to become a serious option *for* the world, it must be visibly and imaginatively embodied *in* the world" (emphasis

28. Hutchings, "Online Churches," 165.
29. Larson, "CyberFaith."
30. Stone, *Evangelism after Christendom*, 12.

original).[31] A church, therefore is being authentic if it is proclaiming and enacting the reign of God, even if in a partial sense. This is much easier to do in physical community than it is digitally, because there are times when we need to show up. We need to show up at justice marches. We need to show up in hospital rooms. We need to show up at city council meetings in order to advocate for our homeless neighbors. We need to show up to accompany an undocumented person to court. We need to show up to embody the reign of God, but social media can help to share the ways that God's reign is present *in* the world.

Conclusion

There are some very interesting trends in autonomous digital faith communities. These groups see themselves as providing a community for those who participate. Whether real relationships are built in these communities remains to be seen. It does seem clear that these communities at least augment the faith of people who are already engaging in offline faith communities. A key point of this chapter is that both autonomous digital communities and social media accounts of brick-and-mortar churches must remember that authenticity is key to growth and the development of real community. People—especially younger people—are leaving the church because of an authenticity problem. The church has done a poor job of practicing what it has preached, and people have noticed. Using social media as a tool to show a community—imperfect though it may be—striving to authentically follow the teachings of Jesus has great potential to bring people back to the church. In the next chapter, we will further explore how a congregation can be authentic by having clearly defined values and using those to guide digital presence.

31. Stone, *Evangelism after Christendom*, 12.

Chapter Three

Values and Social Media

Introduction

CHAPTER 2 ARGUED THAT authenticity was key for the growth and vitality of both online and offline communities. However, in order for a congregation to be authentic, it must know its values. This chapter will argue that clarity of congregational values is directly related to the efficacy of a congregation's social media account. We will examine how to create clear values, ensure that those values translate to social media, look at examples of how congregations have done this well, and suggest strategies for application.

Who Are You?

If you were to ask any given congregation if they knew who they were, they would likely answer with a resounding, "Yes, of course we do!" However, if you asked them to define what that meant in practice, the results might show that they don't know exactly what niche they fill.

Or perhaps different people in the congregation might say different things. I can think of many congregations who have not put forth the effort of fully thinking through how their values translate into practice. I once served in a congregation in a city that was considering removing protections for LGBTQ+ people in the workplace. I was involved in some of the organizing to help keep the protections in place and was amazed at how many faith leaders were reluctant to make public statements. While many would have described the congregations that they served as bastions for radical inclusion and social justice, most were afraid to make public statements, because their congregations hadn't yet gone through the work of discerning their values. While I'm not suggesting that a congregation should have to take a stance on every issue or that a pastor should always speak on behalf of a congregation, I am advocating that a congregation should know the values for which it stands and leaders ought to know how to display those values in public forums.

I used to cringe when I'd hear congregations talking about their mission, vision, and core values. I'd think to myself, "Those congregations are wasting their time in meetings when they could have been doing good work in the world." I also felt like spending time crafting statements was too much of a corporate mind-set coming into the church. "Churches know their mission: to spread the gospel and follow the teachings of Jesus," I thought. The only problem with that is that following the teachings of Jesus isn't easy and it's not always clear exactly what we should be doing. If it were clear, there wouldn't be such theological division in Christianity. I no longer feel like mission and vision statements are a waste of time, as long as they have been thoroughly refined and actually articulate who a congregation is in a very specific sense. Over the years, it has become abundantly clear that people (especially in the mainline Protestant world) have a difficult enough time articulating their own faith, let alone what unique role their congregation plays in the body of Christ. Crafting statements can be a way for congregants to articulate the values for which their congregation stands.

What Do We Stand For, Anyway?

When I first began serving my current congregation, it had been through a very rough period and had lost track of its identity.

While it was still doing wonderful work in the community, the members couldn't articulate who the congregation currently was or who it longed to be. The size of the congregation and the enthusiasm for its future had both declined rapidly. One of the leaders of the congregation who had done a good deal of work in organizational thought and leadership led us through a retreat where we developed the following mission and vision statements. I present them not as perfectly crafted statements that all congregations should follow, but as ones that have worked extremely well for our congregation in developing unity and clarity around our purpose.

> Mission Statement: University Christian Church (Disciples of Christ)/United Church of Christ is a progressive, welcoming, Open & Affirming community that brings people together through worship, love, faith, and service to others by following the example of Jesus Christ.

> Vision Statement: University Christian Church (Disciples of Christ)/United Church of Christ seeks to embody God's inclusive love through creative and vibrant worship and by working toward peace and justice in an ever-changing world.

While both of these statements remain somewhat broad, the mission statement has accurately related the identity of the congregation, and the vision statement has provided a goal of who we want to be in the future. After our congregation developed these statements at a weekend retreat and then passed them unanimously at a congregational meeting, a special team charged with the vision of the church (aptly named the "Vision Team") got to work extrapolating five core values for the congregation, which are listed below. The first sentence of each is the core value and the second sentence reflects how we are striving to apply that value in our context.

1. We are a ***progressive congregation*** that takes the Bible seriously, but not always literally. Doubters are welcome here.

2. We are an ***Open and Affirming Congregation*** that welcomes people of all sexual orientations and gender identities into

the full life and leadership of the church. We are a proud member of the Disciples LGBTQ+ Alliance and were the first Open and Affirming Congregation of our denomination in Southern California.

3. We are a *multiracial/multicultural congregation* that openly welcomes people of all races and ethnicities to help weave the diverse tapestry of our community of faith. We are always striving to be a pro-reconciling/anti-racist congregation.

4. We are an *environmentally conscious congregation* that cares for God's creation and strives to be good stewards of it. We are home to the San Diego Climate Hub, a founding member of the San Diego Green New Deal Alliance, and a Green Chalice Congregation (our denomination's environmental certification).

5. We are a *peace and justice congregation*. We believe that God cares deeply for those who are oppressed and marginalized and make our mission to those in need the center of our ministry.

These values have given the congregation a clear sense of who we are, so that members can clearly articulate what makes us different from other congregations. These values have worked well for us, because there are enough of them to say something substantial about who the congregation is striving to be, while also being short enough to remember. While these core values define who we are, we also realize that they are goals for which we are striving, and many cannot be fully accomplished. I will say just a few words about each value and how that has helped the congregation.

1) Our congregation is part of two noncreedal denominations; as such there is an understanding that members have a responsible freedom of belief. Our first core value that this congregation is *progressive* acknowledges that people are free to interpret Scripture for themselves, but that as a community and from the pulpit, we will embrace a progressive Christian approach to faith. Holding this commitment as a core value helps people know what to expect whenever they enter the sanctuary for the first time. 2) The fact that we are *Open and Affirming*, our denomination's

LGBTQ+ certification, indicates that our congregation has already decided that we will be open to people of all sexual orientations and gender identities/expressions and that we will be affirming of them both inside and outside of the congregation. It also gives me, as pastor, the freedom to speak out on LGBTQ+ justice and inclusion issues on behalf of the congregation. 3) Like many mainline congregations, our congregation has always been predominately White. In embracing our denomination's call to become more *multiracial and multicultural*, we have diversified our congregation. This is one of those core values that is important to strive towards, while recognizing that there's always more work to be done. I take pride in knowing that at the time of this writing, I haven't hired a single straight White man since I began serving this congregation, and of our twenty-three staff members, I am currently the only straight White man. 4) We decided to articulate that we were *an environmentally conscious congregation* because we had recently gone through the process to be certified as one through the denomination. This led to renovation of current facilities and modification of cultural practices to become more environmentally sustainable. We also worked with an outside partner to help move all of the major environmental justice organizations' offices in San Diego onto our campus to create a "Climate Hub." Leadership was adamantly in favor of creating this hub, because it fit in with of our core values. 5) The clarity of articulating that we are a *peace and justice congregation* has allowed us the freedom to speak out about a number of issues that might have been controversial in other congregations. For example, we were able to host a training and worship service before a nationally covered march to the border to protest treatment of migrants. I didn't have to ask for permission from the congregation—nor did I receive any pushback—because pursuing peace and justice is one of our core values.

Of course, just because an organization has done the work of developing these tools for identity and vision, it doesn't necessarily equate to follow-through. In fact, one of the biggest issues with crafting mission/vision statements is that people often spend more time developing the statements than they do actually trying to live into them. Considering the fact that these statements and plans developed from them often have poor follow-through in congregations, many people have dismissed them as a corporate intrusion into the church (as I once did) and an ineffective model of ministry.

In an article about his denomination's use of mission/vision statements and core values, religion scholar Terry Brensinger suggested that core values go back long before the time of the corporate model invasion in churches. He suggests that Leviticus 25 expresses a vision that there should be a Jubilee Year every fifty years (or so), when all debts would be forgiven, and property would be returned to its original owners. From that vision statement, one can imagine core values, such as "social structures that allow every Israelite to flourish," "the welfare of the entire Israelite community over the prosperity of select individuals," and "obedience to God, even when it requires self-denial and sacrifice."[1] These sound like wonderful core values and a great vision statement for what the ancient Israelites would have liked to happen, however as Brensinger points out, there is no evidence that a Jubilee Year was ever actually practiced.[2]

Simply creating mission/vision statements and core values says nothing about how they can be realized in any meaningful way by an organization. Brensinger suggests that core values must be engaged and not simply developed and then left alone if they are going to be meaningful. In speaking about his own denomination, he makes an argument for three steps following the creation of core values that are relevant for all organizations. He suggests that organizations 1) ought to have some idea of expected outcomes from their core values; 2) develop a strategic plan for how those outcomes will be realized; and 3) assess after a period of time if those outcomes have been achieved.[3] In my own experience, re-evaluation and continued discussion of values is often the most difficult part. However, if a congregation makes a commitment

1. Brensinger, "Revisiting," 61.
2. Brensinger, "Revisiting," 61.
3. Brensinger, "Revisiting," 61.

to engage with their values and their mission/vision on a regular basis they can be a very effective means of realizing and living into congregational identity.

Socializing Your Values

While organizational issues like crafting mission and vision statements may seem unrelated to social media, they are, in fact, deeply intertwined (or at least they should be). As discussed in previous chapters, there has been an increasing amount of research on why people are leaving the church. There has been much less written, however, on how congregations can effectively address some of the reasons often cited for the decline, such as irrelevance, increasingly busy schedules, lack of inclusion, hypocrisy, etc. As suggested throughout this book, I believe that one important tool that congregations can utilize to combat decline and instigate growth is social media. Unfortunately, many congregations have not gone through the work of discerning who God is calling them to be and that is often clear on their social media accounts. Simply put, if a congregation doesn't know who it is or why it's there, it won't have an effective social media presence. I follow congregations from all over the country on a variety of social media platforms and the congregations that have the best, most active, most engaging social media feeds are the congregations that have a clear identity and mission.

Many churches' social media feeds don't have much direction. They seem to have a smattering of occasional pictures snapped on someone's phone (often from some event with little description, leaving outsiders to guess what had even happened), occasional memes of Bible quotes, and maybe sermon videos (frequently with poor video and audio quality). With such an approach, it's difficult to discern much about a congregation or its values. Social media streams don't have to be professionally curated to be consistent and authentic, but they do need to be managed strategically and they need to convey the values of the congregation.

Very little has been written on how or why churches ought to convey their core values on social media, but I believe it is essential. Joe Teo is the CEO of the social media planning and collaboration company HeyOrca. Teo discusses the importance of "brand values," which we might translate into the nonprofit world as core values. He says, "Brand values are different from a company mission/vision statement. They communicate your brand's identity, moral alignment, and personality more than mission and vision do. They represent the personality, moral values, and core principles that guide a company."[4] It's unfortunate that oftentimes companies have spent more time reflecting deeper on who they are and why they support the causes that they support than does the church! Teo also says that brand values "provide a reason for why a company does something, like support a non-profit or run a social responsibility campaign."[5] He argues not only that these values ought to guide how an organization uses social media, but that the values should be the specific focus of a social media campaign.

How many churches try to support every cause that comes their way, just because it seems like a "good cause"? Wouldn't it be more effective if the cause fits with a core value and could be highlighted on social media in that way? One example of how our congregation has tried to embrace this idea is by supporting an HIV/AIDS hospice home in Tijuana called Albergue Las Memorias. It is supported by our Global Ministries arm of the denomination, but it is especially important to our congregation because many of the residents who live in the home are LGBTQ+ identifying. Our congregation helped the hospice home to build a dorm specifically designated for LGBTQ+ people and the congregation rallied around the idea, because it was helping us to live more fully into our identity both as an Open and Affirming congregation and a peace and justice church. We partnered with the San Diego Gay Men's Chorus in this effort and it was a powerful way to bring different communities together. The building of the dorm was something that both the

4. Teo, "Share Your Brand."
5. Teo, "Share Your Brand."

chorus and our church social media accounts were able to share as a way of showing that we were living out our values.

Why is this effective? Teo suggests that having a social media campaign that is directly focused on your values gives people a reason to care about and feel an affinity for the organization. Along this line, focusing on values helps to develop a "brand personality" or an overall persona of the organization that helps people to relate to it in a more personal way.[6] Publicly showing that a congregation is practicing what it preaches is a way of confronting one of the most oft-cited reasons that people leave the church—hypocrisy. Every time the church can tell the story of authenticity, it provides a counternarrative to that which is predominant in our culture and is leading to church decline.

It's important to recognize that all of this talk about "branding" might make us uncomfortable. After all, the church is not a brand but the conveyor of a sacred truth we hold dear. However, it is true that to communicate this truth on social media, congregations must be cognizant about how they are portraying themselves and what values they are communicating. If a congregation has spent time actively discerning who God has called them to be in the world, then developing a social media approach that allows people to understand who they are can be an effective way to draw them to the church. I should also make clear that since I come from denominations with congregational polities, I necessarily assume that each congregation will be different from another, while relating to the whole body of Christ and consider that to be a good thing! I recognize that other Christians may have less emphasis on congregational autonomy and individuality. However, even in denominations with less emphasis on individual congregational personality, individual congregations still have ministries that are unique to their setting; those ministries ought to be highlighted.

In the next section, I will look at two congregations that are using social media as a very effective tool to communicate how they are living into their expressed values. They are successful, not simply because they are good at sharing information about

6. Teo, "Share Your Brand."

God, but rather because they know who they are and are allowing their values to influence how they live out the gospel within their particular contexts. Both congregations clearly define their values, they live into them, and they showcase this correlation on social media. Such an approach lifts up the ministries in inspiring ways that other forms of media cannot. In doing so, they strengthen their ministries, bring people into their congregations, and help people to experience God's presence.

How Do Congregations Use Social Media Effectively?

One of the largest and fastest growing congregations in the United Church of Christ is First-Plymouth Church in Lincoln, Nebraska. Their values are clearly stated on their website. They claim to be "Christian, open minded, spiritual, evolving, and diverse."[7] They don't just list these values, they specify what they mean (and don't mean) by each term. For instance, in defining the term *Christian*, Senior Minister Jim Keck states, "'Christian' means we perceive in Jesus the divine qualities of love, peace, joy, and justice. It does not mean we think Jesus is the only path to God."[8] In that simple sentence, the church has laid out its Christology, commitment to interfaith work, and respect for different interpretations of Jesus' life. About being open-minded, Keck states, "We understand faith as a quest, not a clutched certainty."[9] This statement clarifies that the approach of the congregation is one of journey, not of destination. About being spiritual, he says, "We believe God is a spirit of love that can be felt and known by each one of us."[10] This explains that God is immanent and knowable through love. About evolving, he states, "Rather than resisting change or innovation, we eagerly experiment with new ways of being faithful

---

7. Keck, "Who We Are."
8. Keck, "Who We Are."
9. Keck, "Who We Are."
10. Keck, "Who We Are."

and new understandings."[11] Here, he's acknowledged a rootedness in tradition, while embracing new ways of being church. Finally, about being diverse, he says, they "celebrate the differences among [them] such as sexual orientation, ethnicity, class, mental abilities, physical capabilities, personalities, and backgrounds."[12] Here, he explicitly explains who is welcome in the community.

These values are not simply statements about who they claim to be, but rather are clearly lived out as seen when visiting their Facebook feed. Their feed almost exclusively consists of church events and messages from the pastors, which assures consistency of message and the "brand personality" Teo described. The values that they articulate on their website are not merely talking points, they are clearly at the center of what the church says and does. The reflections from the pastors and the themes of the worship services and music show these values at the heart of what they say and do. All of the pastors' messages fit into those expressed values and there are frequently messages about diversity, inclusion, and love. The messages from the pastors also show the congregation's commitment to being an evolving congregation, because they talk about the different types of services that are available at First-Plymouth—some traditional, some not. The very fact that they've invested so heavily in social media shows that while they value tradition, they aren't afraid to adapt; their online community is very much a part of the church. While First-Plymouth doesn't tend to post much about events outside of the life of the congregation, it is clear that its values are lived out within the congregation's life.

Park Avenue Christian Church (The Park) is a congregation of the Christian Church (Disciples of Christ) and the United Church of Christ in New York City. While the congregation is considerably smaller than First-Plymouth and has a smaller social media following, it has a social media page that has clearly reflected its values. On its website, it has a clearly expressed mission and vision. In part, their statement reads, "The community at The Park is on a mission and has a vision—a vision for a more

11. Keck, "Who We Are."
12. Keck, "Who We Are."

just, sustainable, vibrant and growing community that has a broad impact on our city, our nation and our world."[13] Their social media accounts reflect this desire to have an impact outside of their local community. For example, there is a video on their Facebook page called "Restoring Religious Freedom" in which The Park's Senior Minister Kaji Doušа and a lawyer representing her in a lawsuit against the Department of Homeland Security, US Customs and Border Protection, and US Immigration and Customs Enforcement make a statement about the suit and why they are pursuing it. In the statement, they say:

> We learned in March of this past year [2019] that the Department of Homeland Security had compiled a list of people, it included journalists, activists, advocates, lawyers, humanitarian workers, all people who—for one reason or another—had traveled to the Southern border, and specifically to Tijuana, to provide services of all sorts to migrants, to people who were seeking refuge in the United States as part of the Migrant Caravan. And we learned of this government watch list or targeting list, through a whistle blower—someone who worked for ICE, and was deeply concerned by what he saw. The notion that our government would target lawyers and reporters and aid workers because of their interests and the services they were providing to migrants. And one of the things we learned through this list is that there was one member of the clergy on this list. Pastor Kaji from The Park is the one faith leader who was included on this list . . . and so, the lawsuit is in its early stages, but will go on—the government will be forced to produce more documents, we've sought an injunction, which is a court order, to stop the government from targeting Pastor Kaji, to undo whatever it is that has been done as a result of her inclusion on this illegal, unconstitutional targeting list, and to restore her religious freedoms in full.[14]

13. Park Avenue Christian Church, "Mission and Vision."
14. See Doušа and Jones, "Restoring Religious Freedom."

This post is a great example of how the congregation is living its professed value of having an impact on the nation and the world. In the video, they describe how Douša was in Tijuana to help marginalized migrants get married and how she was put on a government list for participating in these activities. With the support of the congregation, she is now suing several government agencies, which has caught national media attention and has been profiled on their social media accounts. This congregation is not all that large, doesn't have a huge staff, but is using their social media to help tell the story of how they are living out their mission and vision in an effective way. Therefore, social media has become a significant tool for them to tell their story.

The Park also states in their mission/vision statement that they "dare to DO ministry in such a way that reaches and impacts the upper east side, the city of New York and beyond with the radical claims of the gospel of Jesus Christ through our worship and our witness as we strive to build and model the beloved community of God."[15] It's important to note that this part of their statement also points to having an impact outside of their local community. Another time that The Park used social media as a tool to have an impact was in 2018 when they invited forty ministers from around the country to participate in a "Gospel According to Hamilton" series. The videos of the sermons were all shared on social media and now have a landing page on The Park's website.[16] These ministers were to preach a sermon inspired by one of the songs in Hamilton, to send it to Park Avenue so that it could be published on the landing page, and to raise funds for "The Hispanic Federation," a nonprofit created by the father of Lin-Manuel Miranda (creator of *Hamilton*).[17] This creative endeavor was an innovative way to use social media as a tool to connect congregations from different denominations (to have a national impact), to examine a cultural phenomenon (to use worship as a way to be relevant), and to raise

15. Park Avenue Christian Church, "Mission and Vision."
16. Park Avenue Christian Church, "Gospel According to Hamilton."
17. Park Avenue Christian Church, "Gospel According to Hamilton."

money for a nonprofit helping people in Puerto Rico to recover from a hurricane (to create the beloved community of God).

How Can Churches Implement Effective Social Media Strategy?

In her book *The Social Media Gospel*, Meredith Gould draws on Bill Gates's aphorism, "Content is king."[18] She states that without content, not much of anything can happen on social media, because people have to have content with which to interact. One thing that all successful social media accounts are doing is sharing content frequently. Some are creating their own and some are sharing content that has already been created, but by doing so on a regular basis, these churches are establishing a presence in people's lives and giving people an opportunity to interact. Both First-Plymouth and The Park mostly create original content that specifically relates to their faith communities. They use pictures, videos, messages from the ministers, and events to create engagement and a sense of community. They also post at least once every day, but usually multiple times per day. While they have media personnel on staff, even congregations with limited staff could implement a similar strategy with a bit of planning.

Churches should have plenty of content available to them. Congregations have events all the time that with a bit of forethought could be publicized on social media. Is there something special going on in worship? Are there guest musicians? Is there a worship focus out of the ordinary or a sermon series that might appeal to the outside community? Is there a special meal or activity? If there's nothing exciting to advertise, perhaps a church could create an event with the outside community specifically in mind (Beer and Hymns is a great event that often appeals to the outside community). By the end of any given week, hopefully pastors know what they're going to preach about and any pastor with a webcam could talk about worship for thirty seconds to a minute to

18. Gould, *Social Media Gospel*, 40.

create a shareable post. Everyone in the congregation has a camera in their pocket on their smartphones; there's likely at least one who has a knack for taking artistic pictures and could share a few with the pastor or social media manager each week (or at least on special occasions). Perhaps there is even someone in the congregation who is an amateur photographer with a higher quality camera and who enjoys producing photographic content to help tell the story of a congregation.

All of the above ideas should be relatively easy for a congregation to implement and give the congregation original content to share, so that people can get a feel for the personality of the congregation. However, it's also a reality that many pastors will be doing this work by themselves. Facebook allows pages to schedule when a post will be published, so that whoever is managing a page could sit down and schedule a week's worth (or as much as a person wants to schedule) of content at a time. While not all social media platforms allow for this, there are a whole host of media scheduling platforms—paid and unpaid—that allow for the scheduling of content across platforms. If a social media content manager—even if that person is the pastor—could set aside an hour a week to schedule posts, they would likely find that the investment of their time was well worth it. Pastors should probably also consider thinking about creating elements of their sermons that would be shareable. When crafting my sermon for the week, I try to think about whether there's a sixty-second or less portion of the sermon (to meet Instagram's requirements) that we could cut and share on social media and link to a full video. Crafting the sermon in this way can draw people into the sermon and may help them watch the whole thing.

Creating and Curating

There are different types of content that churches can use on their social media accounts. Gould points out that while those who create content are called "content creators" and those who find content that's already been produced are called "content curators," many churches both create original content and share content that already exists.[19] Whether a church shares original content or content that has already been produced, it must be meaningful. Gould states, "In the world of the church, we need to create and curate content in the joyful hope of sharing the Gospel, ministering to others, and developing community."[20] I would take this a step further and say that it's not enough to simply share the gospel, because that won't necessarily create a meaningful social media presence that leads to church growth—after all, all faith communities ought to be on social media. Instead, churches must ensure that both the content that they create and the content that they curate not just share the gospel, but demonstrate how their particular faith community is living out the gospel in their own unique context. Showing that a congregation is living out the gospel is how congregations minister to others and develop community on social media, which leads to church growth. When a congregation practices what it preaches, it has finally embraced true evangelism.

It would be nearly impossible for most faith communities to post several different original content posts each day, which is why curated content can be an important tool. If the person who runs a social media account is an avid social media user who follows similarly minded religious accounts, it's relatively easy to share or repost content that reflects their congregation's values. One good example of a congregation that does this exceptionally well is St. Alban's Episcopal Church in El Cajon, California. While they have a limited staff (one clergy person is listed on their website, but they also have a "Social Media Coordinator"[21]) and their congregation appears to be relatively small, they have an incredible social media presence. Despite their size, at the time of this writing, their Facebook page has over 23,000 followers![22] They post a combination of original and curated content, though the vast majority of posts are curated. Since the majority of their audience likely has limited

19. Gould, *Social Media Gospel*, 51.

20. Gould, *Social Media Gospel*, 51.

21. St. Alban's Episcopal Church, "Leadership."

22. St. Alban's Episcopal Church Facebook page.

connection with their physical community, it makes sense that original church-specific content gets less interaction than curated content on their account. They also clearly schedule multiple posts to appear at the same time, and with high frequency throughout the day, so that they will have a strong likelihood of appearing in their followers' newsfeeds. St. Alban's is a good example of how a small congregation can have an impact on a larger audience through good content management. It's unclear if their large social media following has done anything to grow the physical congregation, but they have the potential to have a significant impact far beyond those who gather in the sanctuary on a Sunday morning.

Gould specifies that it's not enough just to post, but that posts must be quality content that "easily and consistently generates interaction in the form of blog comments, 'likes,' retweets, and repins."[23] Obviously, it doesn't do much good to post if the content isn't something that people are interested in seeing. Congregations should experiment to see what kind of content gets the most results and cut content that isn't appealing. Gould also suggests that "quality content will enhance your audiences' knowledge, deepen their understanding, strengthen their faith, stimulate conversation, and build community."[24] That's no small task to ask of content! The faith communities highlighted in the last section, however, are communities that have quality content, which has served to do all of the above.

It's also not enough to post quality content; it must also be posted at the right time and an account must publish the right number of posts each day. Most social media platforms provide analytics that allow publishers to see when their audience is online (and a whole host of other demographics about followers), which enable pages to discern what to post and when to post it. Still, it can be a bit of a task to figure out exactly how often to post. Digital marketing agency Media Cause suggests that the following post rates have been found to be most successful: Facebook: 1–4 times per day (depending number of likes); Twitter: 3–10 times

23. Gould, *Social Media Gospel*, 52.
24. Gould, *Social Media Gospel*, 53

per day; Instagram: 1–2 times per day; Snapchat: 1–2 times per week; LinkedIn: 1–2 times per day.[25] Although these posting rates aren't static, using them as a general guide may help congregations discern which platforms they have the bandwidth to realistically manage. Since I manage the social media accounts for our congregation, I decided that I could realistically manage an Instagram and a Facebook account (our videographer manages our YouTube page) and that I would make a commitment to posting at least once per day. Once I got into the rhythm of doing that, I discovered that our post engagement went up significantly and it was perfectly manageable, especially with the help of scheduling services.

Conclusion

A congregation's mission, vision, and core values are essential. Congregations ought to know who they are so that they can have effective ministry both within their local communities and also online. If congregations have not gone through the effort of clarifying who they are and for what they stand, it's unlikely that they will be able to clearly articulate who they are in a meaningful way online. Congregations that let their statements about who they are guide their social media feeds tend to have an impact that is significant and often goes far beyond their local faith community. Moreover, congregations that express their mission and vision online help followers to have a clearer sense of who the community is and those followers will be more likely to visit. Effective congregations also highlight the ways that they are living out the gospel in their context through worship, service to others, and events. Photos and videos of those activities are often effective, especially if they convey how a congregation is living its values.

Through a bit of planning, even smaller congregations can have a significant impact online. By posting consistently and strategically, a congregation can gain followers. If those posts fit into the mission, vision, and core values then those followers who

25. Gardiner, "Best Practices."

engage with posts from the congregation ought to care about what the congregation is doing and will be more likely to support the congregation in some way. I have found that by posting content that is consistent with our congregation's expressed values, we have gotten followers who had limited or no connection to our congregation. Many of the people then began attending worship (either in person or on our livestream), because the values that we espoused online were consistent with the values that we lived out in the life of the congregation. Moreover, they could see that we were practicing what we preached, so to speak, because we posted pictures and videos to prove it.

Living out the values of the congregation across a manageable number of social media platforms is important to quell church decline and to foster church growth. However, one of the reasons that we are seeing decline in record numbers is because the church, as a whole, has not done a great job in anticipating the future. The church has been reactive rather than proactive (and it's reacted *very* slowly). In the next chapter, we'll explore trends in social media to see what congregations need to be prepared for to keep pace with the rest of society, so that they might have effective evangelism in the future.

— *Chapter Four* —

Changing Churches

Introduction

CHURCHES MUST USE SOCIAL media as a tool to reach others. As has been demonstrated, however, it cannot be a haphazard effort. In order to be effective, congregations must know who they are, be authentic to who they claim to be, and display that authenticity in a unique way on social media. This chapter will examine how a congregation can share its story using social media. It will also call on congregations to be forward-thinking and nimbler than they've been, while examining current social media practices and trends to be on the forefront of digital outreach.

Church Culture and Technological Change

Perhaps you've seen the meme that has floated around on social media of a red car. The car is compact and missing doors in places where you might expect them. The front of the car is where the side should be, and the wheels are facing the opposite direction. The picture is captioned, "Actual photo of a car designed by a church committee." Churches often do incredible work, but it's no surprise to anyone who's ever served on a church committee that the process of decision-making can be slow and the results can be less than optimal. Don't get me wrong, hearing the perspectives of others can be incredibly valuable and in the right environments can foster creativity. Unfortunately, church committees can also be places where people who feel disempowered in other parts of their lives tend to try to assert some control in often unhelpful ways. In an attempt to be "nice" and make everybody happy, committees (and churches, in general, for that matter) tend to propose solutions that don't really address the core issues. A committee structure that slows the rate of decision-making to a crawl is one of many problems in traditional church structure that prohibit congregations from making decisions in a timely fashion. In such a system, it's not terribly surprising that churches are almost always behind the curve of the rest of society.

Churches also tend to be late to the game because new generations are not taking over leadership of the church. Research continues to show that younger generations simply leave the church altogether. Since churches are growing older, congregations are likely to reflect the values and interests of the generations who comprise them, as well as the communication styles. When I first began pastoring my current congregation, the average age of members was considerably older than it is now. I remember that when I proposed switching from using a paper calendar to a digital one, it was as if I had said that we were going to stop reading from the Bible during worship. It was blasphemy! Of course, everyone got used to it and ended up enjoying being able to check the church calendar from their smartphones.

Churches are countercultural places, but often for the wrong reasons. Churches tend to be places where people can go to experience what life might have been like in the 1950s had there been considerably fewer people in worship. Old ways of relating to each other are holding congregations back. Congregations are supposed to be local manifestations of the universal church. Therefore, they should stand apart from the rest of culture and not simply become a social club. Churches are different from other social organizations, because they ought to be a foretaste of the radical hospitality, inclusive love, and transformative justice that God promised through Jesus. Unfortunately, most often congregations miss the embodiment of God's reign and instead cling to a bygone past. But congregations can be countercultural in ways that are authentic to the gospel, while also reaching out to a society in which people's lives are saturated by technology.

Throughout this book, I have been advocating for adoption of social media as an integral part of how a church operates. I believe that churches can be taught how to use social media effectively and can develop a culture where thinking about social media is simply another facet of ministry. To be clear, while social media involves the use of technology, making decisions about how a congregation uses technology in worship itself is a different conversation entirely and a bit out of the reach of this book. While congregations must adopt social media to survive, I'm not convinced that congregations have to integrate screens into their worship to survive. While I think it's important to document what is happening during worship with pictures and video, I also think that congregations can thrive while rejecting projectors and embracing hymnals. While the congregation that I serve has found it valuable to utilize video and projection for worship, if it's not authentic to the worship style of the congregation it may be better to leave it out. There are arguments to be made on both sides of the debate, but my general rule is that if it enhances the worship experience it's valuable, but if it detracts from worship, then it isn't helpful.

Regardless of how individual congregations decide to use technology corporately during their worship services, they should get comfortable with people having their phones out during worship. Congregations should also help people navigate how they use those phones in helpful ways during the service. Whether church leaders like it or not, people will have their phones with them and will likely use them during the service no matter how many disapproving looks are shot their way. Our congregation has a video that runs before the service suggesting ways that people can use their phones during the service that are beneficial for them and the congregation. We suggest that people use their mobile devices to follow us on each social media platform, check in to church on social media, share and interact with others on the livestream of the service, look up the Bible passages we are discussing that day, post quotes from sermons or liturgy, and take videos/pictures of portions of the service that they find meaningful to share on social media. We also remind them to ensure that their phones are silenced as a courtesy to others. In doing this, we acknowledge that technology is a reality of people's lives, while also teaching them how to utilize their devices to share the good news. If people are using social media to show how the congregation is living into its values and making a difference their lives, it can lead others to come into the church and to experience God's presence for themselves. Pastors should also learn to make peace with the fact that some people need to be doing something other than just sitting in the pew to really be able to listen to what's going on during the sermon. I have no issue with people on their phones during my sermons, because I think that people can be on their phones and also listen to what's happening during the service.

The changing reality of how we relate to each other both inside and outside of worship is inevitable. Christians ought to receive a foretaste of the reign of God within the walls of a congregation, but the church should also help us think about how we are called to behave in the world. If churches have nothing to say about something as significant as social media, which permeates most congregants' everyday lives, it has failed to be relevant to the culture in which it finds itself. I'm not arguing that the church ought to simply give in to culture, but rather that it must be nimble enough to show how ancient truths about God's unimaginable love, extravagant welcome, and radical peace are still relevant (or perhaps, even more relevant) to a culture that is too often self-obsessed, money-consumed, and power-hungry. Proclaiming the countercultural message of the gospel on social media can provide a beacon of light and a ray of hope, if only the church will recognize the realities of the current age instead of living in denial.

Part of the blessing and challenge of social media is that it is constantly changing. This can make it difficult for congregations with a notoriously slow model to keep up with the trends, especially if there are no digital natives (Millennials and Gen Z) in church leadership (or even in the church). Throughout this chapter, we'll examine current trends in digital media and look at developing trends of which congregations will need to be cognizant if they are going to thrive. Simply put, congregations must not only be on social media, they need to be utilizing it in relevant ways and anticipating what is coming.

What's Happening in Digital Media Now

As detailed in the previous chapter, congregations need to assess what social media platforms they have the bandwidth to keep up with on a regular basis and to manage well. That means that most congregations will not be on every social media platform. However, congregations do need to keep up with the trends of the platforms they utilize, because they continue to evolve. In order to keep things dynamic, each social media platform is constantly tweaking. Sometimes these have minor effects on pages. An example of this is when the layout of the administrative page of an account changes slightly. However, sometimes the changes can affect the way that people interact with your account altogether. An example of a major impact is when Facebook changed the way that the newsfeed worked, so that the posts that users saw were based on usage algorithms rather than simply seeing the most recent posts. When Facebook made the change, pages then needed users to actively follow their page (beyond simply "liking" it) and interact with it more often to even be able to see the content that they were posting. Major changes like a newsfeed modification impact the strategies that churches need to use to reach people and to make their content relevant. Next, we will examine several current trends that impact how churches should be using social media now.

Live Video

Live video is important for people using Instagram and Facebook. It's helpful because whenever a page goes live, followers get a notification, which makes them more likely to pay attention. Churches ought to be livestreaming their services, but they can also make effective use of live videos to convey short messages. QuickSprout, a digital consulting firm, suggests that 82 percent of users say that they would rather watch a live video than read a social media post.[1] That's understandable, because video is more engaging than an static image and certainly more so than text. With smartphones, it's easy for churches to go live when they're having events or for pastors to go live and invite people to worship. Really all it takes to begin using live video is recognizing an opportunity and pulling out a smartphone to capture the moment. I frequently go live when I'm speaking at a press conference or participating in a justice march. These types of events are good opportunities to let people see the public work of the church that sometimes members of the congregation don't know about and, in doing so, to display authenticity. If you can have professional videographers film with high-end equipment, that's even better!

Hashtags

Companies have discovered that when their customers talk about their products on social media, it's free advertising. It's especially helpful when said customers use hashtags that lump posts together. QuickSprout tells the companies that they work with to push the use of hashtags.[2] Churches should be doing this, too. While it's great whenever people post about the congregation, it's even better if a post helps others learn more about the church and see other posts about the congregation. Tagging the church is important and using a hashtag allows others to see what else the congregation is doing.

Churches probably ought to have a general congregational hashtag and hashtags for special events. For example, our congregation set up a photo booth for families to use after our service

1. QuickSprout, "Top 10 Social Media Trends."
2. QuickSprout, "Top 10 Social Media Trends."

on Easter Sunday. It was extremely popular, and we asked people to use #ucceaster when posting on social media. By doing so, not only did we get people to post their pictures, but it was easy for us to find all the pictures posted and to learn more about guests who were visiting. Churches can use all of the free publicity that they can get, and hashtags are a good way (especially on Instagram and Twitter) to help others learn about the church.

Stories

Ephemeral content, short-lived content that automatically disappears, was once limited to Snapchat. It's so popular that it has infiltrated the big three platforms (Facebook, YouTube, and Instagram). For Facebook and Instagram, ephemeral content comes in the form of stories. *Social Media Today* suggests that using polls or doing videos right before events and publishing them as stories can be particularly effective ways to boost audience engagement or to capitalize on FOMO (fear of missing out).[3]

Churches might consider using a video on stories shortly before an event to remind people that it's coming up. Since it will disappear, a reminder video doesn't need to be as polished as other videos on a church's feed. The video will serve its purpose in a way that won't clutter a feed and people might watch. Congregations also might consider using stories to take a poll on a theological issue or topic for a sermon series as a way to foster user engagement. Stories are also a great place to experiment with content. Since stories are temporary there's more freedom when trying new content to see how people engage with it. If a congregation hasn't been using stories, now is the time to start.

Private Engagement

Messaging is a very important part of social media that is often forgotten when considering how people interact with each other

3. Rendler-Kaplan, "Social Media Trends."

on social sites. I've found that people in my congregation like to communicate in different ways: some will only talk on the phone, others will only reply to email, some want a text, and a growing number want to communicate on messaging apps via social media. Providing pastoral care via messenger is certainly not a class that I had in seminary, but it's a reality of ministry in the twenty-first century! Digital scheduling service Hootsuite suggests that messaging will continue to play a large role and that organizations will need both public (on their public social media feed) and private (messaging) engagement. In an article about upcoming trends, Hootsuite authors Christina Newberry and Sarah Dawley report that research indicates that two-thirds of American social media users say that messaging apps are where they feel most comfortable sharing.[4] That's extremely important information for churches, which specialize in helping people relate their story to God's story. Not much has been written on the benefits of or cautions surrounding pastoral care via messaging, but it is certainly a reality. Benefits for caregivers include being able to respond when they have time to help a person deal with an issue and having a record of a conversation (which can be valuable but should also inspire caution). For the care seeker, it can provide an added way to reach out when in need. For many people messaging will likely not provide the same level of care as actually speaking, so pastors should be prepared to plan an in-person meeting, if they feel it's necessary.

Social media platforms are realizing how important private messaging services are and are beginning to invest more in them. Newberry and Dawley say that in 2019, "Instagram launched Threads, a camera-first messaging app to connect with close friends. LinkedIn began rolling out Teammates. It's a new feature that helps users better connect with people they work with in real life. And Mark Zuckerberg announced plans to unify Messenger, Instagram, and WhatsApp."[5] All of this suggests that while we tend to think of social media as public communication, private communication is becoming increasingly important. This trend

4. Newbury and Dawley, "Trends to Watch."
5. Newbury and Dawley, "Trends to Watch."

indicates that churches will need to find ways to encourage private messaging on their accounts.

While messaging is certainly a growing trend, private engagement on social media can also include closed groups on Facebook. Groups and pages serve different roles. Pages are public and should primarily be geared toward those outside the congregation, while groups are private and can have more internal dialogue. Facebook groups can be a place to exchange prayer concerns, to have a more private digital Bible study, to plan church events, to let members of a small group at the church communicate with each other, etc. This kind of communication can be very valuable and can foster development of community more easily than a public Facebook page. Newberry and Dawley suggest that organizations should be creating pathways from public to private channels to deepen engagement.[6] This isn't a new concept for churches, since the most successful churches try to get people connected with a small group as soon as possible, so that newcomers can begin to develop relationships immediately. The more connected a person is to a community, the more likely they are to stay involved. However, I doubt that many churches have made the connection that this kind of relationship building can happen in the digital world, as well.

Video Conferencing

While video conferencing services are typically not lumped into the social media category, video conferencing is related to the previously described private engagement on social media. Video conferencing is a powerful tool of which many churches—at least prior to COVID-19—were not fully taking advantage. By utilizing this technology more fully, churches can build connection in new ways. Recently, our congregation partnered with the North American Interfaith Network (NAIN) to host a digital conference. People from all over North America got on a Zoom call to attend the conference that then had three presentations in physical locations

6. Newbury and Dawley, "Trends to Watch."

and there were digital breakout groups. This was an incredible way to allow people to attend a conference that would have been inaccessible for many if it had taken place in a traditional conference format. Our congregation is currently planning another digital conference on transgender leadership in the church, which will create shareable video content for social media.

Beyond conferences, video conferencing can provide congregations with a way to remain connected to people who live far away. Due in large part to the cost of living, San Diego tends to be a place where people live for a few years and then move. We have found that people often want to continue to stay involved with our congregation, even after they have moved away, because they still feel a strong affinity for the congregation. While people can, of course, watch our livestream when they move, we've also begun to allow people to continue serving the church while living in a different physical location. For example, we had one member who moved to a different state yet remained on our Financial Accounting Committee because he had valuable expertise and was able to use video conferencing equipment to join our meetings.

One of the challenges that our congregation faces in Southern California is that it can be difficult for people to make it to evening meetings and events because of traffic. However, with a bit of creativity it would absolutely be possible to do a Bible study or church planning meetings via video conferencing instead of asking people to drive to the church. Perhaps churches that are struggling with having enough people involved in church leadership can strive to find easier ways for people to be engaged, like making meetings or events accessible from their homes.

Trends to Anticipate

In the previous section we looked at current trends taking place in social media. However, congregations also ought to be aware of what is currently gaining momentum so that they won't be taken by surprise.

TikTok

For the past couple of years when our congregation has taken our teens on youth trips, TikTok (formerly Musical.ly) has been a popular pastime for our youth. I first noticed them using the app when it was time for the youth to go to bed. As often happens on such trips, long after the adults are ready to go to sleep, the youth had their phones out and continued to use them. When I told them that they needed to "stop Snapchatting and go to bed," I was quickly corrected! I realized how out of touch I was, because they weren't using Snapchat, they were using TikTok. On that trip, whenever there was a short lull in the work, phones would come out and TikTok would be opened.

What is TikTok? About themselves, TikTok says, "TikTok is the leading destination for short-form mobile video. Our mission is to inspire creativity and bring joy."[7] TikTok uses short videos often paired with music to help users express themselves. In writing about the app for the *New York Times*, Kevin Roose says that it's more fun than other platforms, which is why it appeals to the younger generation. He says, "TikTok—a quirky hybrid of Snapchat, the defunct video app Vine and the TV segment 'Carpool Karaoke'—is a refreshing outlier in the social media universe."[8] It's unique among social media sites, Roose states: "There are no ads. There's no news, unless you count learning about viral dance crazes. There are few preening Instagram models hawking weight-loss tea, and a distinct lack of crazy uncles posting Infowars clips."[9] TikTok is enjoyable because it's a bit of a haven for users to have fun without some of the negative side effects of other social media sites, such as echo chamber politics and the negative impacts on mental health that come when comparing one's life with another's. Perhaps this is why Roose says, "About an hour after downloading TikTok, the popular video-sharing app, I experienced a bizarre sensation, one I haven't felt in a long time while on the internet. The knot in my

7. TikTok, "About."
8. Roose, "TikTok."
9. Roose, "TikTok."

chest loosened, my head felt injected with helium, and the corners of my mouth crept upward into a smile. Was this . . . happiness?"[10] More and more people are using this app, and as of April 2020, there were 800 million users.[11] This means that, although it gets less press, TikTok has more users than Twitter, Snapchat, LinkedIn, or Pinterest. Perhaps it's not such an outlier after all.

This app is becoming very popular and it's easy to see how it could become the next big social media site. In an article for *Business Insider*, Paige Leskin states, "If you need proof that TikTok is the wave of the future, look no further than 'Old Town Road,' the mega-hit song of the summer, which got its start on the app."[12] TikTok only came to the US in August 2018 after merging with Musical.ly, but by October 2019 had 1.2 billion downloads (which doesn't necessarily relate to the number of users, since one user might download on multiple devices).[13] Leskin puts it bluntly: "If you're not already on TikTok (or at least familiar with it), you're already behind."[14] Its growing significance was demonstrated in June 2020, when many of the platform's users coordinated to reserve tickets for a Donald Trump presidential campaign rally in Tulsa, Oklahoma. These users had no intention of actually attending, they just wanted to raise expectations and create disappointment when there was a significantly lower turnout than expected.[15]

A few months ago, I wouldn't have recommended that congregations invest much time in TikTok, but it's an increasingly important platform, especially since TikTok videos can also be shared on Instagram. Many of my congregation's most popular videos on social media are not overly serious videos that try to convey heavy theological points, but rather fun videos that teach people something along the way. Perhaps there's an opportunity

10. Roose, "TikTok."
11. Statistica, "Social Networks Worldwide."
12. Leskin, "Guide to Tik Tok."
13. Leskin, "Guide to Tik Tok."
14. Leskin, "Guide to Tik Tok."
15. Lorenz et al., "TikTok Teens."

for churches to think about how TikTok might be used to create promo videos for worship that are short and fun to watch.

According to social media service Hootsuite, around 70 percent of TikTok's users are between the ages of sixteen to twenty-four.[16] Therefore, if a congregation decides to adopt use of this platform, the route that seems to make the most sense is with youth groups/young adults whose members are already using Tik-Tok. Perhaps these groups could use the platform as a part of their youth activities. This would mean that they wouldn't have to suffer through church activities until they could catch a five-minute break to escape the drudgery through TikTok, but rather could use the platform as a part of the activities themselves.

Regardless of whether churches embrace this particular platform for any official use, it's important for congregations to be cognizant of the fact that their young people are very likely using TikTok and prefer it to other sites. It's also important to recognize that its popularity is growing quickly and many social media analysts suggest that it could change the way that we think about social media, especially as it continues to be more video-driven and less text-dependent.

Augmented Reality

Augmented reality and virtual reality technologies are advancing at a tremendous rate and are finding their way into daily social media usage. Lyfe Marketing suggests that face filters (which change the look of someone's face in real time) are now common on most social media platforms.[17] Augmented reality also allows for people to see what physical spaces are like without actually being there. Virtual reality is similar, but a bit more immersive.[18] One can see this technology beginning to become mainstream as people are able to take 360-degree pictures that allow others to interact with

16. Newberry and Dawley, "Social Media Trends."
17. Lyfe Marketing, "Ahead of the Competition."
18. Lyfe Marketing, "Ahead of the Competition."

a picture or for users to take 3D pictures. It's not too big of a leap to see how this could soon become a fully immersive experience.

As discussed in a chapter 2, Second Life for the past several years has allowed users to go to church in an environment similar to that of a video game. As technology continues to develop, it could be that people are able to feel like they're actually worshiping in a congregation's space through virtual reality while in the comfort of their own home. While I wouldn't necessarily advocate for the early adoption of this technology, pastors and congregational social media account managers should be aware that some people already worship in digital environments and this technology continues to develop and gain popularity. If congregations are beginning to engage with people online now, they might be more fully prepared for a possibility of worship in virtual reality in years to come. The thought of worshiping in virtual reality may seem far-fetched, but the technology is already available and as it begins to become more affordable and makes its way into social media platforms, it is very likely that forms of augmented reality will become a part of daily life.

Conclusion

Since many churches have limited bandwidth, it makes most sense to invest time, energy, and money into the networks where they are most likely to see results. This means investing in networks where they are likely to find their target audience. Facebook, YouTube, and Instagram continue to be the big three and are probably the most important places for all congregations to have a presence. As of April 2020, Facebook had close to 2.5 billion users, YouTube had 2 billion, and Instagram had 1 billion.[19] Other popular social media sites currently have significantly fewer users. Twitter has 386 million, Snapchat has 398 million, LinkedIn has 310 million, and Pinterest has 366 million.[20] By numbers alone,

19. Statistica, "Social Networks Worldwide."
20. Statistica, "Social Networks Worldwide."

it's clear that the big three are the best places to invest resources. They also probably best reflect the desired demographics of church outreach. Meredith Gould points out that older generations (Silent and Baby Boomer) use Facebook most, while younger generations (Millennial and Gen Z) use Instagram, Snapchat, Twitter, and YouTube, and the middle generation (Generation X) using a wide variety of platforms.[21] Based on current figures, if a congregation uses Facebook, Instagram, and YouTube they are likely to have an access point for all generations. Concentrating on using these well is likely a very helpful strategy.

It's also important to have a consistent personality and feel of content across platforms. For this reason, it's logical for a single person or media team who understands a congregation's values to manage the platforms. Sometimes churches with limited staff or with pastors who have less interest in social media consider turning their social media over to the youth. They think that since younger people tend to use social media more frequently that it's a good idea to hand the social media over to them. That, however, likely isn't the case. While it's true that it can be beneficial to speak to younger people about what's going on in social media, it's probably not a great idea to entrust your congregation's primary outreach tool to a teenager. Even if teenagers have a good feel for how to use a platform, they likely won't have thought about how to best appeal to a target demographic or how to convey a consistency of brand across platforms. It's not a bad idea to have regular conversations with youth, perhaps even as a part of youth activities, about what's trending in social media, so that congregations with limited staff and less media savvy can remain aware.

Congregations should not assume that what has worked well in the past on each of the big three platforms will continue to work. Since social media is always changing, congregational approaches need to be dynamic. Congregations would do well to pay close attention to trends on social media and to do their best to be early adopters. Current trends like the use of stories, creating space for more private interaction, focusing more on video, and cultivating

21. Gould, *Social Media Gospel*, 17.

conferencing options are practical steps that congregations can take right now. Trends will, of course, change very quickly, but if congregational social media account managers are actively paying attention to trends, they can attempt to help their congregation stay a little ahead of the curve so that the accounts remain relevant.

It's also important for social media account managers to recognize which platforms current congregants use, to have thought strategically about which platform their desired audience is using, and to be thinking about which platforms and technology they ought to be watching. While it's true that churches probably don't have to be early adopters of platforms that fewer people use, it's also true that churches are almost always too late to the game. Consistency is extremely important, as is maximizing bandwidth, and the more social media presence a congregation has, the more likely it is that people will be able to find and learn about who the congregation is and what it values.

— Chapter Five —

Finding Hope

Introduction

THIS BOOK HAS ARGUED that once church leaders embrace social media as a tool, discern their identity, and find a way to tell their story authentically, they've taken concrete steps to bring people into their congregation and to help them experience God's radically transformative love. This chapter focuses on how congregations can get started by acknowledging the importance of social media and taking a few practical steps.

There's Still Hope!

Think about a congregation that you know that is struggling. What is their social media presence like? Are they making an effort to reach people online? Think about a vibrant congregation that you know. What is their social media presence like? Is it easy to find out information about their services and events? Social media is not the end-all and be-all of church, but I can guess that with few exceptions the answer to whether dying churches have a thriving social media presence is "no" and the answer to whether thriving congregations do is "yes." Congregations must continue to live out the gospel in their communities and beyond, because this world is in desperate need of the good news of God's reign that congregations ought to embody. However, the church has always needed to be nimble in order to reach those in new places. Whenever Christianity has spread to new regions, missionaries have learned new languages and have learned about cultures. Their work has allowed Christianity to take on new forms so that it can be adapted to different contexts.

Likely because of the fact that Christianity has been such an integral part of American culture, American Christian congregations got used to people showing up on Sunday mornings simply because going to church was expected. Sure, some churches were larger than others, but there was an expectation in many parts of the country that if a person stopped going to one church, they'd probably immediately find another. I grew up in a Midwestern town where one of the first questions you'd ask someone was "Where do you go to church?" Church membership was simply assumed. This is, of course, no longer the situation for American Christianity. And now, if people stop going to church there's a good chance that they won't be coming back. Just as missionaries who spread Christianity into new regions needed to learn about the culture that they were trying to reach, so do American Christians need to reevaluate the culture in which we live. Traditional forms of evangelism no longer reach people in the same way.

The continued movement of American society away from congregations as the primary gathering place should not come as a surprise to anyone who has been paying attention over the past four decades. I'm not sure that this is such a bad thing, though. Many congregations had become more American social institutions than they were communities embodying the radical gospel of Jesus Christ. The movement of people away from the institutional church has forced congregations to struggle with how to live authentically into the communities that they are called to be. There is, in fact, good news for American Christian congregations: if they are willing to change, they are not doomed to irrevocable irrelevance and eventual death. With effort and a clear sense of purpose, congregations can provide a meaningful path for people to walk on their spiritual journeys. Christian leaders simply need to acknowledge the reality that the religious landscape has changed and be willing to adapt. If they are not willing to embrace new forms of being church, then their fate has been sealed.

However, we know that most people who leave organized religion do not stop believing in God, they just no longer find the church to be a meaningful place to nurture their spirituality. Seventy percent of Americans still consider themselves to be Christian, even though people go to church less than ever.[1] Moreover, only 3 percent of Americans claim to be atheists, while around 4 percent are agnostic and about 23 percent are religiously unaffiliated (the famous "nones" or the "spiritual, but not religious" crowd).[2] Those who are agnostic and religiously unaffiliated could well be open to the message of churches, especially if those congregations are willing to address issues that have caused people to leave church. Congregations can be intellectually honest and be truly open to the questions that people bring with them to church. Christians can strive to live more authentically in their lives together and not be simply "Sunday morning Christians" (where they act one way on Sunday morning and a different way during the rest of the week). Congregations can make more of an effort to be welcoming places to all of God's children. If churches become places that nurture authenticity and God's radical welcome, people may just find that local faith communities can be meaningful mediators of spirituality once again. The "nones" and those who are "spiritual, but not religious" may find that while hiking in nature is a great way to experience the divine presence, there's something to be said for struggling with the meaning of life's big questions within a community, too. People may find that being spiritual and religious are not as dichotomous as they seem at this particular moment in history. Simply put, *there's still hope!*

1. Pew Research Center, "Religious Landscape Study."
2. Pew Research Center, "Religious Landscape Study."

Social Media as a Source of Hope

As I've argued throughout this book, a significant source of the hope comes from social media. While many churches have been slow adopters of social media and some have been rightfully concerned about possible negative mental health impacts, churches can be a positive influence on people's lives and can share the good news by embracing digital media. If people are going to be on social media anyway (and we know that they are) shouldn't the church be there as well to be a source of hope? Many faith communities are beginning to come to terms with the fact that social media is an integral part of twenty-first-century evangelism that is not going away. In a poll cited in a previous chapter, LifeWay Research found that 84 percent of congregations had a website and 84 percent had a Facebook page, while 16 percent used Twitter and 13 percent used Instagram.[3] It's safe to say that the majority of these churches likely do not have effective accounts and it's unfortunate that so few are on Instagram, but the fact that the majority of Protestant churches have a web presence shows the recognition of the need to become relevant to a digital age.

A few years ago, I walked into the congregation that I now serve in San Diego when I was visiting for the first time as a candidate to become their pastor. I looked around at the smattering of people in the large sanctuary and wondered about the fate of the congregation. The people were kind and hospitable, but would the congregation survive? Over the past several years their numbers had steeply declined, and their story looked destined to be the same as that of so many congregations: dwindling numbers and eventual death. But they did not want to die! They wanted new life . . . and luckily that's the central story of our Christian faith. When the congregation called me, they weren't sure of their identity, but they knew that God wasn't done with them yet. After just a few years, the congregation's story is very different; it is thriving. While a lot has happened to change the direction of the congregation, I think most people in the pews would point to social media

3. LifeWay Research, "Pastor Views."

as a large part of what has happened to our congregation, in part because many of those who are sitting there found us online. We clarified our mission, vision, and core values, then we told people about who we were. We didn't just use social media as a tool to tell our story, though—we also invited others to be a part of that story. Our congregation is now serving as a counternarrative to that of church decline, as we continue to see growth and new life.

Yet, the story of University Christian Church in San Diego doesn't have to be an isolated one, because a quick glance at our social media accounts shows how attainable a vibrant social media ministry (and congregation) can be. We are not a huge church, but the congregation is thriving. If someone were to go onto our congregation's Facebook page, they'd see that at the time of this writing, we have just over 1,000 "likes." On Instagram, we have around 500 followers. On YouTube, we have fewer than 500 subscribers. In social media terms, that's a relatively meager following! Yet week after week, we see the results of an investment in social media. Every week people come into the sanctuary and talk about how they've been inspired by what we're doing online. We continue to gain a digital congregation of people around the country who watch our service online and consider our congregation their church home, even though they never—or rarely—step foot onto our physical campus (many of them support the work of the church financially, as well). A digital community has developed on the livestream of our worship service each week. At denominational gatherings, I frequently have people who I have never met offline talk to me about things they have seen our church doing on social media. All of this is to say that a congregation doesn't have to be huge to see the benefits of social media; it simply needs to decide that investing in social media is a priority.

Practical Steps to Get Started

Once a congregation has begun to realize that developing a social media ministry is important, there are practical steps that it can take to begin implementing a more effective online presence. Based on the research presented throughout this book, I propose five initial steps to help churches live into their ministry on social media.

First, congregations should clarify their mission, vision, and core values. Chapter 3 argues that if a church doesn't have a strong sense of identity it won't be able to have an effective ministry. If a church doesn't have a clear identity, not only will it not have an effective ministry on a social media platform, it won't have a clear ministry in its community. How can a church thrive if it doesn't have a clear sense of why it's there? How is the church any different from a social club? A church must be able to articulate who it is, who it's striving to be, and what it holds sacred or it will not have a thriving social media presence. The most successful social media accounts are ones that accurately reflect the identity of congregations. How can a congregation demonstrate its relevance to its community on social issues if it hasn't bothered to think about them? How can a congregation demonstrate authenticity (which is one of the most sacred principles for those who have left the church), if it doesn't know what it means to be authentic within that particular community of faith? Clarifying identity needs to be the first step.

Second, congregations should assess how much bandwidth they have to create quality social media accounts and select appropriate platforms. As stated in previous chapters, part of the congregation's selection process ought to be discerning the target audience. If they're reaching out to Gen X and above, Facebook is the right place. If they're reaching out to Millennial and younger, Instagram is right. On YouTube, a congregation could theoretically reach all generations. Ideally, congregations should probably strive to be on all of the big three social media networks: Facebook, Instagram, and YouTube, and they should also be thinking about utilizing TikTok. Other social media networks are not as essential for churches at this time unless a congregation has sufficient staff to help manage the accounts and to create specific content appropriate for each platform.

Third, congregations should strive to post quality content regularly on each social networking site. The following guidelines were suggested in chapter 3: Facebook: 1–4 times per day; Twitter: 3–10 times per day; Instagram: 1–2 times per day; Snapchat: 1–2 times per week; LinkedIn: 1–2 times per day.[4] A good starting place is to commit to posting at least once per day on Facebook and Instagram and once a week on YouTube. A social media account manager can tell if the content is quality content based on whether or not people are interacting with it. If they aren't, it's best to experiment with different kinds of content. Congregations should probably strive to balance curated content (content created by others) with original content that the congregation creates itself. Account managers should also be looking at the analytics available on most social networking sites to figure out the best times of day to post and to discern what demographic is engaging with posts.

Fourth, while curated content is often more shareable, a congregation's original content ought to help people learn more about the congregation. There are a number of ways that congregations can go about creating original content. 1) Graphic design sites (like Canva) are great tools to help create memes with sermon quotes and professional-looking images across social media platforms. These sites are also useful in developing appropriately sized images for each social media platform's specific requirements. 2) There are several media providers that offer customizable content. Our congregation's website host (Sharefaith) produces mini movies that we sometimes customize and share. 3) Taking (good) pictures of events almost always stimulates interest, especially if the account manager can tag people who are in the pictures. Tagging people allows them to see the post, so that they can comment or share, which in turn allows their social media connections to view the post as well.[5] 4) Churches should be video recording their worship services. Audio is fine if a congregation is doing a podcast in addition to video, but as chapter 4 showed, video traffic is the wave of

4. Gardiner, "Best Practices."

5. If there is anyone in the congregation who is a good photographer and who has experience editing photos, asking that person to take, edit, and send the photos as promptly as possible is incredibly helpful. If not, designating a photographer who can still take good pictures on a phone works, too.

the future. Ideally, congregations should be livestreaming (prefer-ably on Facebook Live instead of a website, so it's social) and plac-ing an edited version on YouTube and a (short) highlight video on Instagram. While it's possible to livestream on a mobile device, for quality purposes congregations should probably invest in cameras and a livestreaming system (we use Sling Studio). Congregations might also want to consider designating a certain section of their sanctuary as a photo-/video-free zone, so that those who do not want to appear online have that option.

Fifth, once a congregation has got a handle on the basics mentioned above, it should think about how the current trends in social media might be applicable to its social media accounts. Are there ways to utilize live videos beyond livestreaming a wor-ship service? Are there opportunities to publish stories? Is there an option for people to move into private social media such as messaging and/or groups to develop deeper relationships? Are there hashtags for specific events? Is there a possibility for people who live farther away to connect via video conferencing? When congregations get to step five and begin identifying and adopting current social media trends as a part of their daily social media ministry, they will likely notice that they've developed a vibrant online presence!

Thinking about Priorities

These five practical steps are helpful ways for congregations to get started in social media and to more fully use it as a tool to help share the good news. While these steps may seem overwhelming if a congregation has had a limited (or absent) social media pres-ence, they are absolutely attainable goals. Will they take time to implement? Absolutely. But time is of the essence when thinking about congregational vitality and life. Every day there is news of more churches closing their doors for good and congregations must make an intentional decision to invest in their future and to live into the new life that God has promised. If these steps are too overwhelming, social media scheduling tools make it possible for a church staff member or volunteer to sit down at the beginning of the week and schedule posts so that the majority of the work is already done. Moreover, since Instagram allows crossposting with Facebook, syncing the accounts allows for an account manager to post on both platforms at once.[6]

How do congregations begin to prioritize social media? It starts with clergy. If churches are going to quell the current trends of steep denominational decline, they will need pastors who are willing to embrace a twenty-first-century model of ministry. This model does away with the pastor as the "designated Christian" of the congregation. Clergy should not be the only ones in the congregation going to visit those who are sick or homebound nor should they have to ensure that all programs run successfully. Lay leaders within the congregation need to step up. Pastors don't have to manage a congregation's social media account themselves, but they do need to have a working knowledge of social media and not act as if it doesn't exist. Since clergy are almost always the public face of a congregation, they need to think about how they can help the social media ministry. Clergy who are preaching need to consider how their sermons could translate to social media. They need to think about how pieces of their sermon might be "Instagramable" and they need to communicate those thoughts with their media team. They should also think about worship themes that are approachable for people who have been out of church for a while, maybe even a very long while. They should try to use accessible language that goes beyond religious jargon because new people won't be familiar with church terms.

Once clergy acknowledge the importance of a social media ministry, all church leaders need to begin thinking about how their congregation meets the needs of those outside the immediate worshiping community. All church events should be designed so that they are not only meaningful for people who are already a part

---

6. While crossposting is possible, I should note that social media consultants tend to recommend doing this as little as possible to keep content fresh. Ideally, separate content is developed for each platform, since different types of content do better on different platforms.

of the congregation but also might be appealing to people who are outside of the congregation. Then, everything that the congregation does that is interesting needs to be shared on social media so that people have an opportunity to see the excitement in the congregation. If church leaders are planning meaningful events, it's important to realize that people outside the congregation may be more interested in attending events or helping with social justice work than they are with attending Sunday morning worship; church leadership needs to be okay with that! I've adopted the phrase, "We're glad you're here and consider you a part of our church family." I've found that letting people know you value their presence without further expectations goes a long way.

Achieving the five steps in this chapter may also mean a change in priorities. Pastors in charge of staff ought to assess both how they and the person(s) in charge of publications are spending their time to see if it's really the best use of time to achieve their goals. For example, does the person in charge of publications spend hours a week on a newsletter that only people who are already invested in the church are going to see? If so, that's not the best use of their time. If office staff members are spending a good deal of time producing a publication, it needs to be developed with people outside the congregation in mind. Is this publication appealing to someone outside the church? If so, how and why? How would they see it? If a publication is only going to be seen by people in the congregation, then it should take a very minimal amount of time to produce and energy should be focused on producing something that helps those outside the congregation learn more about what the church is doing.

Most churches still do a newsletter of some fashion, but it's absolutely possible to rework it so that it is compatible with a congregation's growth goals. A study done by the Direct Marketing Association found that even though email is somewhat passé and in-boxes are more cluttered than ever before, businesses that use email marketing continue to have a rising return on investment.[7] While that may seem irrelevant for churches, it actually makes a

7. Van Rijn, "National Client Email Report 2015," 4.

big difference because it means that a traditional church publication can still be valuable if it is reworked a bit. In an article comparing email marketing and social media campaigns, Joe Murray suggests that newsletters can still be effective because they can mobilize those who are more invested. He says:

> The target market in social media can range over hundreds of thousands or even millions of individuals, many of whom may have little or no interest in your business model. Conversely, the newsletter intends to reach a far smaller, yet much more motivated, group of consumers, customers or clients. When properly developed, each approach can be effective in building customer base and brand loyalty. When the two are combined the total effectiveness is noticeably greater than the sum of the two parts.[8]

While most church social media accounts don't have hundreds of thousands of followers, it is a broader group than those who are on an email list. Therefore, even a traditional publication like a newsletter can be of value in email form. However, printing and mailing word-heavy newsletters to members of the congregation is a poor investment of time and energy. Reworking the newsletter into a digital format with a growable LISTSERV and visually appealing format (such as those provided by Mailchimp or Constant Contact) can be useful. This format can mobilize those who are already invested and draw in those who are new to the community by keeping everyone informed about upcoming church events. It is also possible to have these newsletters automatically post on social media platforms so that those who are interested in learning more about the day-to-day life of the church can see them. Churches ought to limit their email marketing, though, because it doesn't take much for people unsubscribe and cross-posted newsletters on social media are not typically very engaging posts.

Assessing how church staff spend time should always be a regular practice of those who do church management. However, it's also frequently true that those involved in church work always

8. Murray, "Social Media Vs. Newsletter Effectiveness."

feel like there's more to do than there is time to do it. Prioritizing a social media ministry will pay off, but it will likely mean that hard decisions will need to be made about traditional church publications and how staff members use their time.

Resources in Appendices

As congregations begin to use social media more, there will, of course be issues that arise. There are some resources in the appendices to help with a couple of anticipated issues. Appendix A contains a sample social media policy. Social media policies are important to help guide a social media account. Such policies help moderators know what kind of content to share and help set expectations for congregants. I've known of several congregations where members of the congregation have started a social media account for their church or ministry without even telling the pastor or church leadership! Congregations need to be proactive in helping to quell this type of behavior. Appendix B contains a sample photographic release form for minors. While people love to see pictures and videos of children and those often get the most traction, we're living in a dangerous world and the church has an obligation to keep its most vulnerable members safe. Congregations should never share pictures or videos of minors without the expressed written consent of parents or guardians. Appendix C contains "The Ten Social Media Commandments" as a helpful way to remember social media strategy.

Conclusion

Christianity has been around for almost 2,000 years and has constantly had to adapt to the culture around it. One of the reasons that Christianity has thrived for so long is that it has been able to give hope to people in every time and place. Some people confuse institutional church decline with the death of Christianity. Statistics show that this is not the case. People who leave the institutional church are still longing for spirituality in their lives. People still say that they believe in God (or that they might believe in God), they simply no longer believe that institutional religion can help them on their spiritual journey. Congregations that desire to embody the radical hospitality, unencumbered welcome, and authentic lives shown to us by Christ have a message that seems to line up with the one that people who leave the church say that they are longing to hear. So we should tell them!

Instead of dying a slow, quiet death, churches need to follow the teachings of Christ in a very public way and invite others to do the same. Congregations need to use social media as a tool to spread the good news. They need to put their congregants to work helping to build the reign of God by liking, commenting, sharing, retweeting, repinning, and inviting. After all, if people are having meaningful experiences in church, if congregants are encountering the divine presence, shouldn't they *want* to share that? The Great Digital Commission has been commanded! We have been called to spread the good news from our doorsteps to ends of the earth using not only our words, but our posts, our memes, our videos, our events, our pins, and our very lives. May it be so.

Sample Social Media Policy[1]

UNIVERSITY CHRISTIAN CHURCH's (UCC) Social Media Policy defines parameters to guide church staff, leaders, and volunteers when social media is used on behalf of UCC or when UCC becomes a part of social media dialogue. What is social media? Social media consists of applications and websites that enable social networking and the creation/sharing of digital content. Since social media is always evolving, this policy applies to all platforms regardless of whether they are specifically mentioned in this policy.

Guiding Principles

UCC's digital presence will be guided by its Mission Statement, Vision Statement, and Core Values.

Mission Statement:

University Christian Church (Disciples of Christ)/United Church of Christ is a progressive, welcoming, Open & Affirming community

---

1. Designed using resources at https://socialchurch.co/social-media-poli-cies-churches-ministries/. All church forms should be reviewed by an attorney before use.

that brings people together through worship, love, faith, and service to others by following the example of Jesus Christ.

Vision Statement:

University Christian Church (Disciples of Christ)/United Church of Christ seeks to embody God's inclusive love through creative and vibrant worship and by working toward peace and justice in an ever-changing world.

Core Values

1. We are a progressive congregation that takes the Bible seriously, but not always literally. Doubters are welcome here.

2. We are an Open and Affirming Congregation that welcomes people of all sexual orientations and gender identities into the full life and leadership of the church. We are a proud member of the Disciples LGBTQ+ Alliance and were the first Open and Affirming Congregation in Southern California.

3. We are a multiracial/multicultural congregation that openly welcomes people of all races and ethnicities to help weave the diverse tapestry of our community of faith. We are always striving to be a pro-reconciling/anti-racist congregation.

4. We are an environmentally conscious congregation that cares for God's creation and strives to be good stewards of it. We are a Green Chalice Congregation.

5. We are a peace and justice congregation. We believe that God cares deeply for those who are oppressed and marginalized and make our mission to those in need the center of our ministry.

Branding

All UCC social media accounts shall conform to UCC's brand guidelines, which are on file in the church office.

Social Media Accounts

Any social media accounts representing UCC should only be created by UCC staff members with the approval of the Senior Minister. All social media accounts will be administered and moderated by the Senior Minister or a designated staff member. Any accounts not meeting these criteria shall be deleted immediately. Requests for closed Facebook Groups for programs of the church should be submitted to the Senior Minister. All ministers shall be members of any UCC group on social media.

Moderator Duties

Moderators of UCC's social media accounts are responsible for ensuring compliance with this policy. All posts should be compatible with the above-stated values. Any comments or threads shall be monitored to ensure that they are also consistent with the expressed values. Moderators are responsible for responding respectfully and deleting inappropriate or disrespectful content. If users post content inconsistent with UCC's values, they may be banned.

Guidelines

- All content shared shall be in compliance with copyright laws.

- Photos and video will be posted on UCC's social media accounts. Moderators will respect anyone who has disclosed that they do not wish to have their likeness represented on UCC's social media accounts. With the exception of children who are leading worship and will be on the livestream, photos/videos of children under the age of eighteen may only be shared once UCC's photo/video release form has been signed and returned.

- Social media posts should never disclose sensitive or confidential information, unless written consent to share said information is obtained from the individual it concerns. This includes but is not limited to personal and/or medical information.

- Other than the Senior Minister, who is authorized by the UCC bylaws to speak on behalf of the congregation, no other staff member or congregant should portray themselves as speaking on behalf of UCC.

- All posts, comments, and responses shall be respectful or they will be deleted.

Negative Portrayal

If you see violations of this policy or you see someone speaking negatively about the congregation, staff, or congregants of UCC on social media, please contact the Senor Minister immediately.

Sample Minor
Photo/Video Release Form

University Christian Church
Minor Photo/Video Release Form[2]

At University Christian Church (UCC) we believe deeply in intergenerational ministry and try to include children as often as possible in worship leadership. We also remain committed to a vibrant social media ministry. As such, if you fill out this form your child may be seen on the church's social media and/or church publications. Thank you for helping us tell UCC's story!

2. Adapted from a form on https://eforms.com/release/photo/minor-child/. All forms should be reviewed by an attorney before use.

Appendix B

I, _____, the parent or legal guardian of _____ [minor] grant University Christian Church my permission to use the photos and/or video of my child for the church's publications and/or social media. If I have concerns about a photo/video that is posted, I will contact the UCC's social media account manager so that the photo/video can be removed.

Parent/Guardian's Signature:

_____ Date _____

Parent/Guardian's Name _____

Child's Name: _____

Phone Number: _____

Email: _____

— Appendix C —

Ten Social Media Commandments[3]

1. **Thou Shalt Publish (At Least) Daily**

   Remember, there are different rules for different platforms, but when getting started, you should publish at least once a day. The suggested guidelines discussed previously were Facebook: 1–4 times per day; Twitter: 3–10 times per day; Instagram: 1–2 times per day; Snapchat: 1–2 times per week; LinkedIn: 1–2 times per day.[4] Content should also vary between platforms.

2. **Thou Shalt Use Multiple Platforms**

   Different people prefer different platforms and preferences tend to be generationally based. Older generations (Silent and Baby Boomer) tend to use Facebook and blogs and younger generations (Millennial and Gen Z) tend to use Instagram, Snapchat, Twitter, and YouTube, and the middle generation (Generation X) uses a wide variety of platforms.[5] Select a platform based on who you want to reach.

---

3. I am certainly not the first person to propose guidelines for social media in the form of a Ten Commandments list—a quick Google search will find several—but based on the research and findings of this paper, I propose my own Ten Commandments for creating a vibrant social media account.

4. Gardiner, "Best Practices."

5. Gould, *Social Media Gospel*, 40.

3. **Thou Content Shalt Reflect Thy Values**

    One of the biggest complaints about churches is that they are hypocritical. Know your mission, vision, and core values and let your content reflect your authenticity; be who you say you are.

4. **Thou Shalt Publish Quality Content**

    You want users to interact with your content. If no one is liking, commenting, sharing, reposting, retweeting, repinning, etc., then you need to adapt your approach.

5. **Thou Shalt Interact with Followers**

    It does no good to post quality content that gets your followers talking if you don't interact with them! Let them know that you care they are there.

6. **Thou Shalt Use Videos and Photos**

    Videos are the wave of the future for social media and photos are quality content for most churches. Post original videos and photos when you can and be sure to tag your followers who are featured.

7. **Thou Shalt "Go Live"**

    In addition to videos that have already been recorded and polished, going live can help to publicize events and generate interest. Congregations should also livestream worship and special events.

8. **Thou Shalt Use Scheduling Tools**

    Posting can feel like a full-time job (and it is for some people). To help it feel more manageable, use a scheduling tool and plan as far out as you are comfortable. Don't be afraid to update content depending on what's going on in your congregation, community, nation, or the world to remain relevant.

9. **Thou Shalt Think of Outsiders**

    Remember, the goal of social media is not just to keep those who are already involved engaged throughout the week, it's to reach new people. Don't use church jargon and try to use content that might be relevant to those interested in learning more about Christianity and your congregation.

10. **Thou Shalt Publicize Events**

One of the best ways to keep people (both inside and outside of the church) engaged is to have events. Leverage social media to promote events. During the event, post something about it. Afterward, share a video, photos, or a reflection so that people know why it was meaningful.

Bibliography

Allison, Dale C. *The Luminous Dusk: Finding God in the Deep, Still Places.* Grand Rapids: Eerdmans, 2006.

Barna Group. "State of the Bible 2017: Top Findings." April 4, 2017. https://www.barna.com/research/state-bible-2017-top-findings/.

——. "What Millennials Want When They Visit Church." March 4, 2015. https://www.barna.com/research/what-millennials-want-when-they-visit-church/.

Blowers, Paul, et al., eds. *The Encyclopedia of the Stone-Campbell Movement: Christian Church (Disciples of Christ), Christian Churches/Churches of Christ.* Grand Rapids: Eerdmans, 2004.

Brensinger, Terry L. "Revisiting Our Core Values: Sentimental Slogans or Compelling Convictions?" *Brethren in Christ History & Life*, no. 1 (2019) 61–69.

Burke, Daniel. "Millennials Leaving Church in Droves, Study Finds." May 14, 2015. https://www.cnn.com/2015/05/12/living/pew-religion-study/index.html.

Campbell, Heidi A. "Understanding the Relationship between Religion Online and Offline in a Networked Society." *Journal of the American Academy of Religion* 80, no. 1 (March 2012) 64–93. https://dx.doi.org/https://doi.org/10.1093/jaarel/lfr074.

Campbell, Heidi A., ed. *Digital Religion: Understanding Religious Practice in New Media Worlds.* New York: Routledge, 2013.

Cheong, Pauline Hope. "Authority." In *Digital Religion: Understanding Religious Practice in New Media Worlds*, edited by Heidi A. Campbell, 72–87. New York: Routledge, 2013.

The Christian Left. "Our Story." https://www.facebook.com/pg/TheChristianLeft/about/.

Douša, Kaji, and Stanton Jones. "Restoring Religious Freedom." Park Avenue Christian Church. December 24, 2019. https://bit.ly/2MwpMuT.

Evans, Rachel Held. "Want Millennials Back in the Pews? Stop Trying to Make Church 'Cool.'" *The Washington Post*, April 30, 2015. https://www.washingtonpost.com/opinions/jesus-doesnt-tweet/2015/04/30/fb07ef1a-ed01-11e4-8666-a1d756d0218e_story.html.

Bibliography

Flatt, Kevin, D. Millard Haskell, and Stephanie Burgoyne. "Secularization and Attribution: How Mainline Protestant Clergy and Congregants Explain Church Growth and Decline." *Sociology of Religion* 79, no. 1 (2018) 78–107. https://doi.org/10.1093/socrel/srx044.

Gardiner, Ian. "Social Media Best Practices for Nonprofits: A Comprehensive Guide." Media Cause, November 6, 2017. https://mediacause.org/social-media-best-practices-for-nonprofits/.

Goffman, Erving. *The Preservation of Self in Everyday Life*. Garden City, NY: Doubleday, 1959.

Gould, Meredith. *The Social Media Gospel: Sharing the Good News in New Ways*. 2d ed. Kindle ed. Collegeville, MN: Liturgical, 2015.

Gryboski, Michael. "Disciples of Christ Continues Decline; Church Membership Drops by Half since 2000." *The Christian Post*, October 17, 2018. https://www.christianpost.com/news/disciples-of-christ-continues-decline-church-membership-half-of-what-it-was-in-2000–227988/.

Hartford Institute for Religion Research. *How Religious Congregations Are Engaging Young Adults in America*. Kindle ed. Hartford, CT: Hartford Institute for Religion Research, 2015.

Helland, Christopher. "Ritual." In *Digital Religion: Understanding Religious Practice in New Media Worlds*, edited by Heidi A. Campbell, 25–40. New York: Routledge, 2013.

Hobson, Katherine. "Feeling Lonely? Too Much Time on Social Media May Be Why." *National Public Radio*, 2017. https://www.npr.org/sections/health-shots/2017/03/06/518362255/feeling-lonely-too-much-time-on-social-media-may-be-why.

Hutchings, Tim. "Considering Religious Community through Online Churches." In *Digital Religion: Understanding Religious Practice in New Media Worlds*, edited by Heidi A. Campbell, 164–72. New York: Routledge, 2013.

Jones, Jeffrey M. "U.S. Church Membership Down Sharply in Past Two Decades." Gallup, April 18, 2019. https://news.gallup.com/poll/248837/church-membership-down-sharply-past-two-decades.aspx.

Keck, Jim. "Who We Are." First-Plymouth Church. 2019. https://www.firstplymouth.org/about-2.

Kendall, Lori. "Community and the Internet." In *The Handbook of Internet Studies*, edited by Mia Consalvo and Charles Ess, 309–25. West Sussex: Wiley-Blackwell, 2011.

Larson, Elena. "CyberFaith: How Americans Pursue Religion Online." Pew Research Center. December 23, 2001. https://www.pewinternet.org/2001/12/23/cyberfaith-how-americans-pursue-religion-online/.

Leskin, Paige. "The Ultimate Guide to Tik Tok, the Hot App Gen Z Is Obsessed with and Facebook Is Terrified Of." *Business Insider*, October 24, 2019. https://www.businessinsider.com/tiktok-how-to-use-short-form-video-app-gen-z-2019-6.

Lifeway Research. "Pastor Views on Technology: Survey of Protestant Pastors." 2019. http://lifewayresearch.com/wp-content/uploads/2018/01/Sept-2017-Pastor-Views-on-Technology.pdf.

Lin, Liu yi, et al. "Association between Social Media Use and Depression among U.S. Young Adults." *Depression and Anxiety* 33, no. 4 (2016) 323–31. https://dx.doi.org/ https://doi.org/10.1002/da.22466.

Lischer, Richard. "The Sermon on the Mount as Radical Pastoral Care." *Interpretation: Journal of Bible and Theology* 41, no. 2 (1987) 157–69.

Lorenz, Taylor, et al. "TikTok Teens and K-Pop Stans Say They Sank Trump Rally." *New York Times,* June 21, 2020. https://www.nytimes.com/2020/06/21/ style/tiktok-trump-rally-tulsa.html.

Lyfe Marketing. "New Social Media Trends That Will Put You Ahead of the Competition." October 18, 2019. https://www.lyfemarketing.com/blog/ new-social-media-trends/.

Masci, David. "What Do Americans Look For in a Church, and How Do They Find One? It Depends in Part on Their Age." Pew Research Center, August 23, 2016. https://www.pewresearch.org/fact-tank/2016/08/23/ what-do-americans-look-for-in-a-church-and-how-do-they-find-one-it-depends-in-part-on-their-age/.

Minear, Paul S. *Images of the Church in the New Testament.* Louisville: Westminster John Knox, 2004.

Murray, Joe. "Social Media Vs. Newsletter Effectiveness." https://smallbusiness. chron.com/social-media-vs-newsletter-effectiveness-48831.html.

Newberry, Christian, and Sarah Dawley. "The 5 Most Important Social Media Trends to Watch for in 2020." Hootsuite, December 10, 2019. https://blog. hootsuite.com/social-media-trends/.

Park Avenue Christian Church. "The Gospel According to Hamilton." https:// www.parkavenuechristian.com/hamilton.

———. "Mission and Vision." https://parkavenuechristian.com/mission-and-vision/.

Pew Research Center. "Choosing a New Church or House of Worship: Americans Look for Good Sermons, Warm Welcome." August 23, 2016. https://www.pewforum.org/2016/08/23/choosing-a-new-church-or-house-of-worship/.

———. "Religious Landscape Study." 2014. https://www.pewforum.org/ religious-landscape-study/.

———. "Religious Landscape Study: Religious Composition of Adults in the San Diego Metro Area." https://www.pewforum.org/religious-landscape-study/metro-area/san-diego-metro-area/.

———. "Social Media Fact Sheet." June 19, 2019. https://www.pewinternet. org/fact-sheet/social-media/.

Primack, Brian A., et al. "Social Media Use and Depression and Anxiety Symptoms: A Cluster Analysis." *American Journal of Health Behavior* 42, no. 2 (March 2018) 116–28. https://dx.doi.org/https://doi.org/10.5993/ AJHB.42.2.11.

———. "Social Media Use and Perceived Social Isolation among Young Adults in the U.S." *American Journal of Preventative Medicine* 53, no. 1 (July 2017) 1–8. https://dx.doi.org/10.1016/j.amepre.2017.01.010.

Bibliography

QuickSprout. "Top 10 Social Media Trends." April 23, 2019. https://www.quicksprout.com/social-media-trends/.

Radde-Antweiler, Kerstin. "Authenticity." In *Digital Religion: Understanding Religious Practice in New Media Worlds*, edited by Heidi A. Campbell, 88–103. New York: Routledge, 2013.

Rendler-Kaplan, Lucy. "6 Key Social Media Trends to Watch in 2020." Social Media Today, December 5, 2019. https://www.socialmediatoday.com/news/6-key-social-media-trends-to-watch-in-2020/568481/.

Roose, Kevin. "TikTok, a Chinese Video App, Brings Fun Back to Social Media." *New York Times*, December 3, 2018. https://www.nytimes.com/2018/12/03/technology/tiktok-a-chinese-video-app-brings-fun-back-to-social-media.html.

Roozen, David A. "American Congregations 2015: Thriving and Surviving." Hartford Institute for Religion Research. 2015. https://faithcommunitiestoday.org/wp-content/uploads/2019/01/American-Congregations-2015.pdf.

Sarner, Moya. "The Age of Envy: How to Be Happy When Everyone Else's Life Looks Perfect." *The Guardian*, October 9, 2018. https://www.theguardian.com/lifeandstyle/2018/oct/09/age-envy-be-happy-everyone-else-perfect-social-media.

Second Life. "Spirituality and Belief." https://secondlife.com/destinations/belief.

Senior, Donald. *The Gospel of Matthew*. Nashville: Abingdon, 1997.

St. Alban's Episcopal Church Facebook page. https://www.facebook.com/StAlbansElCajon/.

St. Alban's Episcopal Church. "Leadership." https://st-albans-church.org/leadership/.

Sidani, Jaime E., et al. "Association between Social Media Use and Depression among U.S. Young Adults." *Depression and Anxiety* 33, no. 4 (2016) 323–31. https://doi.org/10.1002/da.22466.

Statistica. "Most Popular Social Networks Worldwide as of April 2020, Ranked by Number of Users." https://www.statista.com/statistics/272014/global-social-networks-ranked-by-number-of-users/.

Stone, Bryan P. *Evangelism after Christendom: The Theology and Practice of Christian Witness*. Grand Rapids: Brazos, 2007.

Teo, Joe. "Why You Must Share Your Brand Values on Social Media Right Now." October 23, 2018. https://heyorca.com/blog/social-media-planning/brand-values-social-media/.

TikTok. "About." https://www.tiktok.com/about.

Turkle, Sherry. "Connected, but Alone?" TED Talk, 2012. https://www.ted.com/talks/sherry_turkle_alone_together.

Van Rijn, Jordie. "National Client Email Report 2015." Direct Marketing Association, April 2015. https://dma.org.uk/uploads/ckeditor/National-client-email-2015.pdf.

Webb, Marion Stanton. "Church Marketing: Building and Sustaining Membership." *Services Marketing Quarterly* 33, no. 1 (January 4, 2012) 68–84. https://dx.doi.org/https://doi.org/10.1080/15332969.2012.633440.

Bibliography

Wellman, Barry. "Little Boxes, Glocalization, and Networked Individualism."
In *Digital Cities Ii: Computational and Sociological Approaches*, edited by
Peter Van den Besselaar, Moto Tanabe, and Toru Ishida, 10–25. Berlin:
Springer, 2002.

Wells, Samuel. *God's Companions: Reimagining Christian Ethics*. Malden, NJ:
Blackwell, 2006.